THEO AND ME

GROWING UP OKAY

MALCOLM-JAMAL WARNER

WITH
DANIEL PAISNER

FOREWORD BY
BILL COSBY

AFTERWORD BY
ALVIN F. POUSSAINT, M.D.

E. P. DUTTON NEW YORK

Published in the United States by E. P. Dutton,
a division of NAL Penguin Inc.,
2 Park Avenue, New York, N.Y. 10016.

Published simultaneously in Canada
by Fitzhenry and Whiteside Limited, Toronto.

Library of Congress Cataloging-in-Publication Data

Warner, Malcolm-Jamal.
Theo and me : growing up okay / Malcolm-Jamal Warner
with Daniel Paisner.—1st ed.
p. cm.
Summary: The popular teenage television actor uses excerpts
from his fan mail as a jumping-off point to discuss troublesome aspects
of adolescence, including family life, dating, and drugs, with
examples drawn from his own experiences on and off the set
of "The Cosby Show."
ISBN 0-525-24694-0
1. Warner, Malcolm-Jamal.   2. Cosby show (Television program).
3. Teenagers—Correspondence.   4. Television actors and
actresses—United States—Biography. [1. Adolescence.   2. Warner,
Malcolm-Jamal.   3. Cosby show (Television program)] I. Paisner, Daniel
II. Title
PN2287.W43A3   1988
791.45'028'0924—dc19   88-15077
CIP
AC

Designed by REM Studio

1 3 5 7 9 10 8 6 4 2

First Edition

For all of you who took the time to write

Dear David Brokaw, Dan Strone, Barry Haldeman, Bill Cosby, Alvin F. Poussaint, M.D., Leslie Baliff, Ph.D., Larry Klino, Pat Hill, Virginia Jones, Linda Kateeb of the McDade Classical School (Chicago), Mrs. Barrow of Hyde Park Career Academy (Chicago), Flonnie Anderson of the Career Center (Winston-Salem, North Carolina), Bette Carriker of the Northwest Middle School (Winston-Salem, North Carolina), Pamela Warner, Robert Warner, Jr., Meg Blackstone, Marcy Carsey, Tom Werner, Eric Kahan, Miriam Baum, and all of my friends (though you never knew I was writing this book): a big thank you to you all, for all of your assistance, input, and support.

—Malcolm, 18

P.S. Danny Dan (Mr. Paisner). We did it, deadlines and all. Thanks, man.

CONTENTS

★ ix ★

Photographic inserts follow pages 64 *and* 144.

FOREWORD

One thing is sure about this book: whether you are—or have ever been—a teenager or are—or ever expect to be —a parent, you will be better prepared for the experience, emotionally and intellectually, after reading *Theo and Me* by my television son and real-life friend, Malcolm-Jamal Warner.

Malcolm would be the first to admit that he is no expert on psychology or adolescent behavior, but this book is filled with such down-to-earth honesty and common sense that it enlightens while it delights and entertains us. Here you will find the voices of young people from all over the world who write to Theo/Malcolm, as one teenager to another, about their lives and the problems they confront as they struggle to survive that roller-coaster passage from childhood to adulthood.

Since adolescence is one of the most critical and complicated stages of development, it deserves more—and better—attention from those of us in the world of movies, television, and radio. On television, "children's programming" is usually geared to the very young, while "adult programming" most often addresses an audience of people eighteen or older, at least in terms of realistic life situations and opportunities. That leaves thirteen- to seventeen-year-olds in limbo, unaddressed in any meaningful sense. Only relatively recently has television begun to produce programs that confront some of the issues that are important to teenagers. But even these are usually "for" or "about" teenagers; Malcolm's book lets the youngsters speak directly to each other about what's on their minds. It is unusual for teenagers to write to each other as peers about the serious—or even not-so-serious—issues that worry and upset them. (I guess maybe the definition of *serious* depends on whether or not that particular problem affects you!)

Some popular magazines focus on the teenage years, but there is a dearth of material on the subject of run-of-the-mill, normal adolescence. Most of what we find in the bookstores is written by "experts" and directed at parents or other adults who want advice on coping with the "troubled" adolescent. So I welcome *Theo and Me* as a real milestone in this respect.

In fact, Malcolm may have hit on the way to go to reach this age group. As we all know, teenagers usually show a lot of resistance to advice from so-called experts, parents, and other adults in authority—not always, but often enough to make "getting through" to them a real challenge. They do, however, tend to listen to each other, and to be open to the values of their peers.

Psychologists like to say that teenagers are controlled by peer pressure. Maybe so, but that's not the whole story. When you read the letters written to Theo/Malcolm and Malcolm's commentary, you will discover that adolescents have many strong ideas and feelings of their own, and that they cannot be easily stereotyped. Teenagers are not the only ones who are "troubled" or "at risk"; many of the most important issues they struggle with—sex, drugs, alcohol, relationships, depression—are equally important to adults. Even the difficulty of coping with parents does not disappear (many adults face the problems of aging parents who create a different set of demands), but all these issues appear to be more critical for teenagers, who are trying hard to achieve their individual identity and autonomy.

Malcolm addresses these subjects with candor, and he often refers to his own thoughts and experiences. He is not afraid to take on the tough issues of race relations and prejudice, sex and AIDS, teen pregnancy, alcohol and drug abuse. Obviously, he is not a "typical" teenager. Malcolm has, after all, been a star of "The Cosby Show" for the past four years, yet he shares many of the common feelings of teenagers, regardless of their life circumstances. He talks about his own fears and anxieties as well as his triumphs. Much of this book is frankly autobiographical—we learn a lot about Malcolm's life, his development into young adulthood, and his remarkable ability to cope and achieve.

Malcolm has special qualities that all of us, particularly his young admirers, would do well to emulate. I truly respect him for his ability to listen, to take advice, and to learn and grow as an actor and as a person. Early in the book, he talks about auditioning for the role of Theo and, at first, reading the part as that of a streetwise kid. When I asked him if in real life he would react that way to his father, he smiled and said, "no." I sent him out of the room to rethink the attitude his character should take. There were two other boys who were given an opportunity to go out and make adjustments on their characterizations. Malcolm was the only one who more than satisfactorily came back with an interpretation that was right on target, and he won the part.

Malcolm has continued in that spirit. He works very hard at his craft, and he is determined to grow as an actor. We work closely together on the show, and there's good chemistry, even a kind of rhythm, in our interplay. He's a regular guy, and he plays a mean game of basketball! I have heard it suggested that I am a father figure to Malcolm, but that's only the make-believe of "The Cosby Show"; actually, I feel more like an older friend or big brother to him. As you'll find out, Malcolm has a real-life father. While I'll remain his friend and colleague, Malcolm will continue to display the strength of character that comes from his own growth, not from me.

The money and glitter of show business have not turned Malcolm's head, or derailed his values and ambitions. He recently turned down an offer to make a Hollywood movie, opting instead to appear in an off-Broadway production that he believes will help him develop his acting skills. The movie would have paid him many times what he is earning in the play; I don't know too many adults who have the maturity to make the choice that Malcolm did. He plans to finish high school and go on to college—and it seems to me that this is what growing up is really all about. Teenagers who care about themselves and their future will exert effort for their own development, thereby being prepared to meet and take advantage of any opportunity that comes their way.

Malcolm sums up his message to teenagers this way: "There are a lot of things about yourself and your life that you *do* have control over. It's never too late to turn over a new leaf and make the best of what seems like a bad situation." That's all that any of us, at any age, can do, but that kind of attitude is what keeps us alive and growing.

Theo and Me is good reading. It is entertaining, educational, and enlightening—a definite three-pointer for my friend Malcolm.

William H. Cosby, Jr., Ed.D.

1

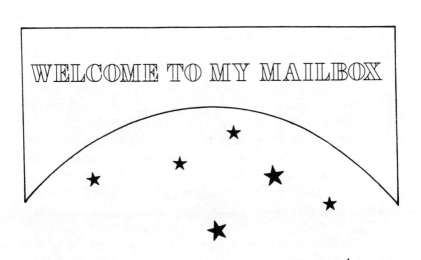

WELCOME TO MY MAILBOX

NOTES ON THESE NOTES

Dear Theo: Got to say you are one of my most biggest fans.
                                                    —*David, 9*

I don't know what it is about myself, but somehow I feel different from many of the people my age. Do you know what that's like?
                                                    —*Le Anne, 17*

I wish drugs never existed.
                                                    —*Trini, 14*

*No one ever listens to me, which is why I'm
writing to you. Maybe you'll listen to me.*
　　　　　　　　　　　　　　—Tammy, 16

You should see some of the mail I get.

Each week the letters come in by the hundreds—on a
good week, thousands—either to the NBC studios in New
York and Burbank, California, or to the offices of Carsey-
Werner Productions, the producers of "The Cosby Show,"
or in care of some magazine or other. Sometimes it seems
I should have my own zip code, there's so much of the
stuff. The letters come in from as far away as Soweto,
South Africa, and Brisbane, Australia, and as close to
home as Brooklyn, New York, and Anchorage, Alaska.
They come from entire classrooms of kids, and they come
from a little girl on a farm in Idaho, twenty miles from her
nearest friends. They come on fancy stationery and they
come on lined loose-leaf paper and they come on the backs
of grocery bags; they're printed on dot-matrix computer
printers and they're written in crayon; some of them come
with friendship bracelets or T-shirts or colorful stickers or
poems or drawings or photographs; some of them even
smell like perfume.

You get the idea.

A lot of times the letters are addressed to Theo Huxtable, the character I play on "The Cosby Show," on NBC
Television, or to all of "The Cosby Kids," but they're also
written to Malcolm, or to Mal-Jam, or to Mr. Warner.
Sometimes the postman finds me with nothing more to go
by than "Cosby Son": no street address, no zip code, no
city. But whatever they call me, and wherever they find
me, the kids who write to me know me as Theo. That's how
we met.

You see, they know me as I appear on television every
Thursday night: a basically good kid who always manages
to do the right thing; but who also gives his parents and
his sisters a little bit of a hard time, who also doesn't like

to study for school, who also has some trouble with girls, and who also would rather do things the easy way or not at all. That's Theo. Through him, they see me as the typical American teenager. My room is as messy on the show as theirs is at home; my character gets into the same kind of trouble that they do; we listen to the same music; we laugh at the same things, and we worry about the same things. Our problems are pretty much the same. I look through the bundles of letters I've collected and I think there has to be something else behind them other than my being a television actor. The something else is that Theo Huxtable is a friend, a true friend, to a whole lot of kids.

And so I get letters. Lots of 'em.

What they have to say is usually pretty standard fan mail stuff: I really love your show (send me an autographed picture); what's your favorite food? (send me an autographed picture); you're one of my favorite celebrities (send me an autographed picture); how did you get started in show business? (send me an autographed picture); I think you're cute (send me an autographed picture). I go through a lot of autographed pictures and I cover a lot of the same ground.

But some of these letters are special. Well, all of my letters are special—keep 'em coming!—but to be honest, the ones that can be helpful to other kids are the ones that interest me most. They're helpful because of what they tell us about growing up and fitting in, and they're helpful because they tell other kids they're not alone. The only trouble is, finding a helpful letter can sometimes be like looking for a needle in a drug clinic (sorry, I couldn't resist), but when I come across one it's always worth the look.

Every once in a long while, then, I'll hear from kids who are lonely or scared, kids who are depressed, kids who are struggling, kids who are reaching out. I'll also hear from kids who are intelligent and insightful and deeply concerned about big things and little things. Some of the letters are funny, some of them are sad, but the point is that a whole lot of kids have got something important to say and for whatever reason they've chosen to say it to me.

Believe me, it's an honor, even if it's an honor I don't always know how to handle.

> *Malcolm, I need a friend. I need a friend in a guy. I have a best friend but now she's away at college. My problem is you need a friend of both sexes. Know what I mean? Because sometimes you need two opinions to a problem.*
> *—Cissy, 15*

> *Do you find it easy to forgive people? I try not to hold a grudge but sometimes I can't help it.*
> *—Nathan, 17*

> *I have experienced a number of family problems in the last two to four years. Examples: I have been beaten until my face was black and blue, degraded until I lost all self-esteem, and put out of the place I called home. My brothers and sisters have the same treatment. It's been pretty bad, but with all the pressures we have been forced to face, I don't give up on my future and dreams of becoming an actress/scriptwriter and become the "low-lifed nothing" my mother always told us we were.*
> *—Latrice, 16*

I'll get letters from kids whose parents are going through a tough divorce, from kids who want to say no to drugs but don't know exactly how, from kids struggling with their own sexuality, and from kids who find the pains and pressures of growing up too much to handle. Once I even got a letter from a mother who asked if I could please talk her teenage daughter out of having premarital sex.

That letter showed me that the pains and pressures of being a parent must sometimes also be too much to handle.

If I had to put a number on it, I'd say that about ninety-five percent of my mail is fun and lighthearted and nothing worth writing books about. It's between me and Theo and the kids who write, and that's where it ends.

This book is about the other five percent. About a year ago it occurred to me that a book plugging into what kids are thinking about and talking about (and writing about) would be a great way for all of us to better understand each other and for our parents to better understand us. Plus, it would be a chance to address some very real problems and concerns that I think all of us deal with in one way or another. This is a tough time to grow up—probably every generation of kids thinks nobody's ever had it quite so hard as it does, and mine is no different. I thought maybe, just maybe, we could use some of these special letters as a mirror, to help see what the rest of us are up to, what we're thinking.

I'm hoping that these letters will show us what we look like.

I feel like I don't belong in high school. At least not in this high school. I'm like an outsider. Most of the other girls in school are into clothes, makeup, and fashion, and spending money. And also boys. They're all so phony. I haven't been really close to anyone here since I've been here. Is it me who needs to change to be accepted or should I just forget about it?
—Cassie, 17

I don't have peer pressure so much as I have parent pressure. My brothers and sister are very popular in school but I realize I never will be in the "in" crowd, and I don't want to be. The trouble is my parents. They keep pressuring me to join things like cheerleaders, debate club, pom-pom team, and everything. It's getting on my nerves.

—Sally, 16

I want to talk to you about a problem that I have. I'm lonely. A lot of kids are lonely; they even have a commercial for it on TV. Maybe you could get your producers to do a show on loneliness.

—Brian, 16

What bothers me more than anything else is the idea most teenagers have that they must pretend to be something other than themselves to impress people.

—Robert, 17

Not all teens are drug addicts. Not all teens are disrespectful. Not all teens lose their virginity before their sixteenth birthday. Malcolm, if you could give just one message to the world for me, tell everyone it's like the saying, "Believe only half of what you hear."

—Marco, 15

As I sit down to write this, I keep thinking of that television commercial—I think it's for some kind of aspirin or something—where an actor steps in front of the camera and says, "I'm not a doctor, but I play one on TV." It's as if we're supposed to trust his medical judgment because of the part he plays on television. Maybe you've seen the ad. Well, that line keeps running through my head right now, and there's another one that runs along with it: "I'm not a teenager, but I play one on TV." But the thing is, I am a teenager. I may work every week on a very popular television show, my picture may turn up in magazines and newspapers, but when I'm not working I'm pretty much like any other kid. I've got problems, just like everybody else: I worry about what I'm going to do with the rest of my life; I worry about fitting in; I worry about girls; I worry my parents. No, I'm not a psychologist or social worker. I'm not in any position to give advice or counseling, but this book is not about advice or counseling. This book is about being a friend, about opening our eyes, about listening. On those subjects I think I'm qualified.

Of course, there are those who'd line up to disagree. They'd even write in. When word got out I was writing a book using some of my fan mail as a starting-off point, I received the following letter:

> *I don't think that you should write this book. I totally think it's a bad idea. It seems to me that your status as a child star makes you think you have something worthwhile to say. I think the opposite is true. Being a teenage "idol" has made your insights less valuable than those of other kids. You drive around in a limo. You drink mineral water, with fruit. What does a TV darling, elevated above society, with no concerns about money, school, friends, attention, or their role in life, know about teenagers today? Tell me that.*
>
> *—Cedric, 17*

Well, Cedric, I think you're wrong. And I think anyone who reads this book will agree with me. First of all, I don't think I'm any better than or different from anyone else. And more important, most of the kids who write to me don't think I'm any better than or different from anyone else. In fact, most of the kids who write to me think they're different from everyone else. That's the whole point. This book is about them; it's not about me. It's about individuals.

It's about *you*.

When I started out on "The Cosby Show," I answered all of my fan mail personally. Each and every piece. I'd sit up half the night sometimes, but I just couldn't see how someone could take the time to write to me without my taking the same time to write back. My friends told me I was crazy, but I didn't think so. I still don't. Of course, the amount of mail I got in that first season is nothing compared to the flood that comes in today. I'm not saying that to brag or anything. It's just that a lot has happened in the past four years; with the success of "The Cosby Show," things have changed. It's happened to all of us on the show, to anyone who's ever been on a successful television show. The fan mail now is just too much for one person to keep up with, particularly with a job and school to keep up with, too, and so I have some help.

But I still ask to see the letters from the kids who are looking for more than just an autographed picture, and this book is my answer to all of those letters with something extra in them, the ones that deserve far more than a standard response. When my friends ask me what this book is about, I tell them I'm writing one big fan letter to everyone who's ever taken the time to write to me. That's the way I feel about it.

Now, these kids didn't write to me expecting their thoughts and problems to be displayed in some book for all the world to see. I understand that and you have to understand I'm not out to take advantage of them. It wouldn't be fair for me to take letters from kids who're reaching out for some kind of help or advice and parade their personal problems on these pages. It would be wrong to take the concerns of kids who are in pain or in trouble and turn them into some kind of object lessons for the rest of us, at their expense. The last thing I want is for some kid to regret writing to me because something he told me in confidence is related in this book in such a way that it could be traced back to him. That's not what I'm about and that's not what this book is about. The kids who write have put a certain trust in me in writing and opening up, and it is not my intention here to violate that trust.

> *You can't tell anybody this, but I went out with this guy recently who was going with one of my best friends at the time. She said she was gonna write to you about it, but I don't know if you got her letter.*
>
> *—Nina, 15*

So, in the interests of privacy and fair play, all of the names have been changed in the letters printed here; where no name was given, I have supplied one. If a hometown is mentioned in the body of a letter, it has also been changed. (The gender of the letter writers, and their ages, when they are given in a letter, have usually not been changed, to help put the comments into some kind of perspective.) Where they appear, identifying remarks and related incidents and ideas within the letters have also been changed to protect anonymity. Often, in the interests of space and clarity, certain themes and ideas addressed in several letters have been compressed into one letter here. Most times I've just taken a line or two from a three- or four-page letter, but sometimes I've pulled slightly longer chunks from even longer letters. In no case does the edited letter represent more than a fraction of the original; in all cases, where the edited letters are not true to the letter of the originals, they are true to the spirit.

That's about all I have to say for now. The rest you'll pick up as you go along.

Here's that line running through my head again: "I'm not a teenager, but I play one on TV . . ."

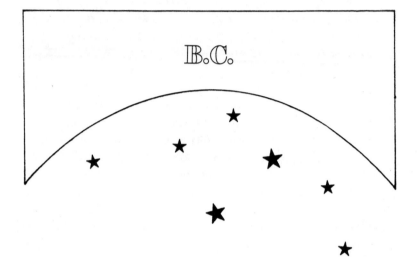

2

B.C.

NOTES ON LIFE BEFORE COSBY

How is it you started in show business? What's it like in there?

—*Gracie, 14*

I read in a Fresh *magazine that you always wanted to be an actor. It said that even before you were Theo you were also some other parts on other shows. True or false?*

—*Larry*

Are you friends with Michael J. Fox or Whitney Houston or Alex Trebek?

—*Alexa, 11*

I know, I know, I said this book was going to take a serious look at some of the stuff on the minds of today's youth. I said I was going to deal with hard issues like sex and drugs and depression and divorce and loneliness and peer pressure. I said I was going to help us to see what makes us all tick. I'll get to all of that, and then some, but first I have some details to get out of the way.

As I said, most of my mail is fan mail. The genuine article. The other stuff, the good stuff (what I've taken to calling "the sex 'n' drugs 'n' rock 'n' roll letters" among my friends), is of most interest to me, and of most interest in a book such as this, but most of the letters are from kids who want to know the basics. They want to know when I started acting, how and when I got my first big break, what my life is like, where and when I go to school, what I'm doing next. They want to know if it's hard work keeping up with school and acting on a television show every week. They want to know what it's really like to work with Bill Cosby. They want to know everything.

Well, this is as good a place as any to tell them.

Any tips for a young guy, like your age, who wants to be a big star?
—Nick, 14

In my school we did a play, it's called Great Caesar's Ghost, *and it's about Julius Caesar and some ghosts and I play one of the ghosts. Maybe if you need ghosts on The Bill Cosby Show, like if Theo is maybe having a bad dream, maybe you can give me a call. I'm a pretty good ghost, anyway that's what my teacher said.*
—Bobby, 11

Once I was on a casting call for a jeans commercial and I got called back three times but finally I didn't get it. Then, like a week later, I got

★ 11 ★

called back for a cereal commercial but it wound up I didn't get that either. Rotten eggs, right? Someday I want to be on a show like yours.

—Katrina, 14

My mother says I can't go on auditions for modeling because it would interfere with school. She says when I'm older I can do what I want, but that now I'm on her time and do what she says.

—Paula, 16

Judging from my mail, it seems that every other kid wants someday to be an actor or an actress or a model. Kids don't want to be astronauts or teachers or doctors or lawyers or cops anymore; they want to be stars. It's a dream to many kids not because they think they'll love the work or the process; they just want to be famous. At least that's what I'm getting from the kids who write to me.

When I started out, acting was nothing more than a hobby to me. A friend of my mother suggested I take an acting class. I was nine years old, and the thing I was into most of all was basketball, but basketball season was over and I needed something to fill my time so I went to check it out. I was looking for something to do outside of school and this class seemed as good as any of the other ideas me and my mom kicked around. It was part of a children's theater program in a community theater up in Inglewood, California, and I had to audition to get into the class. I was nervous, but I must have done okay because I got in.

I started having fun right away. The first thing we did was a play called *Alice Is That You?*, which is a takeoff on *The Wizard of Oz,* and I got the part of the Tin Man. Rehearsals were a lot of fun. A lot of my friends were in the class, and I made some new ones after I joined, and it was like hanging out with your friends. We used to do all these acting exercises and everything, and it didn't seem like work at all. It was just a good time.

Then, when we actually performed the play, I was hooked. People in this business always talk about when they first got bitten by the acting bug; well, for me it was the very first time I was on stage before an audience. Mostly it was the audience that got to me: the way you could get them to laugh or applaud, the way they're paying this close attention to your every move. I liked being the center of attention. The greatest charge for me was my first curtain call. You know, you rehearse for weeks and then you come out on opening night, and people give you standing ovations. Really, if you've ever been cheered by a crowd of people, in sports or in anything else, then you'll know what I'm talking about. Here was this whole group of people, strangers, telling me, loudly, that they appreciated what I did. I remember thinking this was something I could get used to.

Anyway, that play led to another play, this one called *Babes*, which was about a big marble tournament. All of our plays were done with an all-child cast, and most were original productions, and in this one I had one of the lead roles—I'll never forget my character's name: Lolo Lamont Leonard Lawrence Liston, Jr. You have to understand, most of our material was aimed at a young audience (we were, after all, just a bunch of kids ourselves), but our plays were always fun to put on and fun to watch. We always had good-looking costumes and sets. And we'd pack the house. Then after we'd finish our run at Inglewood we'd sometimes take the shows on the road, touring throughout California, and I really started to develop a love for performing.

As far as I was concerned, acting was the next best thing to basketball.

A lot of the kids who were in the class were looking to make some kind of inroads into Hollywood. You'd see a lot of the stereotypical stage moms hanging around at every rehearsal, and they would sometimes make things very tense for the rest of us. To a lot of kids, then, the class was a kind of career move, and they would compete for the best parts and everything. To me, though, and to a lot of my friends, the class was still just an activity, an outlet. You have to understand, I was raised as an only child, and so I always had this active imagination. I'd stage these big battles with my army action figures, or set up elaborate road races with my Matchbox cars. To amuse myself I would always invent these stories to keep myself company, and now I found myself on a stage, which is just another kind of fantasy world.

I was there for different reasons than most kids, but I fitted right in. The class would meet every Saturday, all day, and when we were in rehearsals we'd meet almost every afternoon leading up to the performances. The shows would run for a couple of weeks. Eventually, a small group of us got more seriously involved in the program, and so the teacher (a cool guy named Gary Veney, who eventually became my manager) added another, smaller class for us on Friday nights.

At this point I was really getting into it. Acting was starting to take up a lot of my time. Make that almost all of my time. As I said, for most of the other kids it was a career move; agents and producers and Hollywood types would come to these shows and a lot of kids and their parents thought it was a good showcase. But I was still thinking of the class and our plays as something to do. I never thought about actually going out to do it professionally. That's not just a line; it's the truth. My mom wasn't a typical stage mom; she didn't push me into it at all. In fact, she was worried that I would neglect some of the other things I had to do. She made sure I still did all of my chores around the house, and she stressed that school was my first priority.

Eventually, one of the agents attending the shows told me I had some potential. She wanted to sign me up.

Me and my mom talked it over for a while, but then we decided it wasn't something we wanted to pursue. One of the reasons was that my mom was going to graduate school then, and she wouldn't be able to take me to any auditions, but the main reason was that we thought it would take too much time away from school and some of the other things I liked to do.

That would change.

Well, let us get on with why I wrote this. I would like to be a movie star. Maybe play as Vanessa's boyfriend. Or as a cousin who has come to stay with you for the summer. See what you think.
—Alan, 11

I already have my life planned. I'll finish school, go to college and while I'm at college I'll send a tape to Motown and be discovered. I will finally live out my dreams of becoming a singer, an actress, and/or a talk show host.
—Betina, 15

I always thought of myself as being on television. I probably would not be that good at acting. I really don't know. I mean, I've tried to audition for small parts here and there but I lost all faith in myself and just gave up. I always told myself there is someone better than me and they will get the part. I guess I should not be like that, because I'll never get anywhere like that. I don't have enough self-esteem.
—Mary Eileen, 14

You really do need to feel good about yourself if you want to be an actor. It's a life filled with rejection and uncertainty, and you never know what's going to happen from one job to the next, or even if *anything* is going to happen from one job to the next. Show business is a very self-involved business, and there are a lot of things about it that are pretty tough on kids and adults both. Of course, when I was eleven or twelve years old, all I knew was I was having fun, and when that same agent approached me and my mom again about a year later, this time we signed on. The agent was a woman named Miriam Baum (she still represents me), and right away she started to send me out on auditions.

The first one was for a television show called "Matt Houston." Don't even ask me what the part was, or what the episode was about, but I got it. It was a small part, but it was mine. One for one, right out of the chute. But it didn't go to my head. Not yet anyway. The next thing I was up for was a guest shot on "Fame." My character was in the school choir and two of the regulars taught the choir to play basketball, so mostly all I did was lip-sync to some songs and play some hoops. Actually, I did a lot more than that (I had a featured role in that episode), but the playing ball and syncing were the fun part and so that's what I like to remember. By this time my head was swelling pretty big. It was kind of a big deal to some of the other kids in school, my being on television, and I was like, the world is about me now. I was hot stuff, at least in my own swelled head.

So there I was—two auditions, two jobs—and you just couldn't talk to me. My agent was sending me out only for lead roles (she wouldn't even send me out for commercials), and that also inflated my ego. The acting was still fun, and the classes were still fun, and on top of that there was this success. But then my luck ran out. I was around thirteen, and I was going on audition after audition, and I just couldn't get a part. I went back four times to read for a movie called *The Last Dragon*. They kept saying they wanted a hard street kid, so I went in to my final call-back and there were all these big wigs there—Suzanne De Passe from Motown, and the director, Michael Schultz

—and this time I played the role hard. I'm strutting and I'm grabbing at my crotch, because that's what I thought they wanted. When I was done they were all quiet and they said they were looking for someone a little less street.

With auditions it sometimes seems that you can't win.

Once I auditioned for a part on the television show "Gimme a Break." They were thinking of doing a spin-off with Don Rickles, and I went back to read for the part three or four times. It seemed as if the audition would never end. Things looked good for me for a while, but then they ended up giving the part to a girl. Was I that bad?

But you can't let it get to you. If you're going to pursue this as a career, you're going to miss out on almost every role you're up for. That's right: every role is a long shot. I let it get to me only one time that I can remember. I cried when I missed out on a part on the show "Benson." I don't know why I cried. It was no different from some of the other parts I didn't get, but I remember sitting down with tears in my eyes over that one. I was thirteen years old. Keep in mind, all this time I was keeping up with the plays and my acting classes and with school and with basketball and with my friends. Maybe repeated rejection, on top of all that, is too much for a kid to have to take.

My luck turned on Good Friday in 1984. How's that for timing? I'll never forget it. I went out to the movies with my mom (we saw *Romancing the Stone*) and we were out all day, having a good time. We stopped for something to eat after the movie, did some shopping, and really made a day of it. Well, thank God for answering machines, because when we got back there were four or five messages from my agent and my manager telling me they'd set up an audition for a new television show starring Bill Cosby, who at that time I knew mostly from his Saturday morning cartoon show, "Fat Albert and the Cosby Kids," and from commercials; I didn't even know they'd sent my picture out to be considered for the part.

★ 17 ★

By the time we got back it was after office hours, but everyone was waiting around for me and I was told to rush over to the producer's office for the audition. I still didn't know exactly what the show was about, or what part I was auditioning for, but I raced over there and did a reading with the casting director. It was about six o'clock. I don't remember what the scene was about, but I was in the middle of the audition and the phones just started ringing, three or four at a time, and people were reaching to answer them and I was still going on with the scene. I didn't get distracted, but the casting director did, and so he asked me to do it again and so I did.

Maybe he saw something he liked; or maybe he was just tired, because I was, literally, the last person he was supposed to see (they had already done auditions in New York, Philadelphia, and Chicago); or maybe it was something about the ringing phones that made my performance stick out in his mind, but for whatever reason he asked me to come back the following Monday to meet Mr. Cosby, and to meet the directors, the writers, the whole bit.

I'd been this way before, and so I was only a little bit excited. Getting called back sometimes means only that the rejection will be a little bit harder to take. I had no idea what was coming.

Is Bill Cosby really your father? Is he funny at home the way he is on TV?
—Claudell, 11

Here's what I read. I read that Bill Cosby has all this Jell-O and Coke in his closets because otherwise he'd be in trouble with the police and the government because he has to really use them like he says on the commercials.
—Alice, 12

Working with Mr. Cosby and the wonderful cast must be a true joy for a young actor such as yourself. The show seems so filled with warmth.

—Peggy, 16

Actually, the small room where we all waited to audition the following Monday was pretty much filled with warmth. Serious, competitive warmth: we were all sweating something fierce. They had us set up in this waiting room—all the kids auditioning for the other roles, and the women auditioning for the part of Bill Cosby's wife on the show—and we were all sweating bullets. There were two other guys up for the part of Theo, which was the role I was reading for. There were about three or four actors reading for each part. At this point, the producers and writers weren't sure if Vanessa, the second-youngest child in the family, was going to be a girl or a boy, or if Rudy, the youngest, was going to be a girl or a boy, so they had a mix of kids reading for those parts.

Over the weekend we had learned a little bit about the show. I was reading for a part as Bill Cosby's oldest son on a family situation comedy. The show, which was initially turned down by another network, had a six-episode commitment from NBC. Everyone else in this room was also reading for a part in the same television family.

We were all strangers, hoping to become very closely related to each other, very quickly.

They took us in one at a time. I remember when the other Theos came out they were saying, "I'm sure I got it; I'm sure I got it." There was this whole big psych job going on, which is the way it always happens in auditions, even if you're just thirteen years old. The first time I went in, the room was crowded with the producers and writers and casting people. Bill Cosby and Jay Sandrich, the director, were also there. That was the first time I'd met them. I did my reading and came out saying, "I'm sure I got it; I'm sure I got it," just like the other guys.

Meanwhile, I wasn't so sure.

A while later I went back in, and this time I read a scene, with one of the casting people, between Theo and his father, and I was playing the role the way you usually see kids on television. You know, a real smart-aleck kid, the kind who rolls his eyes when his father is talking, that kind of thing. That's what I see on television, so that's what I did, and I thought I did a great job. When I finished, I looked up at Bill Cosby and he said, "Would you really talk to your father like that?" And I said, "No, I wouldn't." And he said, "Well, I don't want to see that in the show."

That was the first thing he said to me, and I was thinking, Okay, I guess I can go home now. The other guys up for the part are out there saying, "I'm sure I got it; I'm sure I got it," and I'm in here thinking, I just want this to be over so I can go home.

I was with Gary Veney, my acting teacher, and we talked about what happened, and the next time I went in I read the scene totally differently, and this time when I finished I looked over at Bill Cosby and he said, "Excellent, excellent," and then I figured maybe I didn't blow this audition after all. You have to remember, Bill Cosby wasn't this entertainment giant to me, the way he is now to so many people. I knew nothing about that. As I said, I knew his cartoon show and his commercials; I think my mom had some of his comedy albums; and to me he was just this nice, funny man who was looking to put together the best possible cast for his new show. That's all. He wasn't intimidating or anything, and I still don't see him that way. At the time, when he came over to me and told me he liked that I worked on my reading and listened to his comments, I just thought that maybe I didn't act my way out of a job after all. I thought I still had a shot.

After what seemed like the longest while in the history of the world, Jay Sandrich came out into the waiting room and told us how sorry he was that he couldn't just send us all home and contact us through our agents, the normal protocol after an audition like this. He said there just wasn't enough time, and then he was going on and on about how we all did a terrific job, thank you for coming, and I was thinking, hurry up, hurry up, hurry up. Tell me I didn't get the part so I can just go home. And then he said if he calls our name we should follow him into the next room.

So Jay picked Phylicia Rashād, to play Clair; Lisa Bonet, to play Denise; Tempestt Bledsoe, to play Vanessa; and Keshia Knight Pulliam, to play Rudy. (The role of Sondra wasn't created until later in our first season.) I was standing behind him, so he couldn't see me too easily, and he was looking around, and I was feeling it was a little bit like being on the end of the bench in a basketball game, waiting for the coach to make some kind of eye contact so he'd put me in the game, and then he turned around and said he wanted me to come with them too. My first thought was for the two guys who didn't get the part; I felt bad for them. Right away, I remembered how dejected I would feel when I lost out on a part, particularly when I would come this close, and I couldn't let myself believe it or feel happy. I remembered how upset I was that time I missed out on a part on "Benson." I looked over at those two other guys and I couldn't shake feeling bad for them. So in the instant after Jay Sandrich said my name I was speechless and I didn't know what to do and I was frozen and I must have stood there for I don't know how long because I wasn't moving and he finally had to say, "Go, go, go."

At that point I went, went, went because I didn't want him to change his mind. I felt bad for the other Theos, sure, but I wanted the part.

It must be a lot of fun to be on the show, but it must be a lot of work too. Your work shows on the show. But I wonder, is it all work, or is it some acting out real life "teenage" problems? I say this because sometimes on the show I can guess what the next few lines are going to be because I've dealt with some of the problems in my house.

—Anthony, 15

I don't know, if it was me I would miss going to regular school with regular kids. You know, a regular life. Everything for you seems glamorous but I don't know if it's for me.

—Jonny, 14

How is it going to school with Rudy and Vanessa and all? It must be easy if you sometimes have to do second grade stuff with the little kids. I wouldn't mind some of that.

—Andrew, 14

We made the pilot episode out in Los Angeles, and the first big scene I did is still one of my favorites. Maybe you remember it. It was the one between Theo and his father, Cliff, where Theo says he wants to be "regular people" when he grows up and Cliff uses Monopoly money to show how much money it costs for "regular people" to have everything they want. The two of them go back and forth about how much it costs for rent, for food, and for transportation, and before Theo knows what hit him he's left with a few lousy dollars of Monopoly money out of each imaginary paycheck. Even then he thinks he'll be making enough money to have the things he wants, but then all of a sudden Cliff says to him, "Will you have a girlfriend?" and Theo says, "You bet!" and then Cliff grabs away whatever money is left in Theo's hand. That got a big laugh.

It was a funny scene, and it was really the first time I got to meet Theo and figure out what he was all about. He's always looking for a shortcut.

Everyone was pretty pleased with the pilot, and then the next thing we knew the producers started talking to us about relocation money. Me and my mom knew the show would be taped in New York, but we suddenly had to face the prospects of packing up and moving across the country. Now, I was born in Jersey City, which is just outside Manhattan, and we lived there just after I was born until my parents separated, but me and my mom were pretty settled now in Los Angeles. We weren't thrilled about moving back to New York and leaving everything behind in California, and we actually sat down and took some time to think about it. We made a list. My mother would have to quit her job, we'd have to sublet our house, and I'd have to make special arrangements for school and leave behind all my friends. I didn't know any kids in New York, except for some cousins I hadn't seen in years. We didn't know if this job was going to last for six shows or for six years, and we didn't want to uproot ourselves without thinking about it.

Finally we decided to go for it. We didn't think in terms of going beyond the initial six episodes, but we thought even that would be good experience for me. We could always pick ourselves right back up and head back to Los Angeles, and we thought the exposure from those six shows, with Bill Cosby, would be good for my career. It was the first time I started to think of acting as a business, and it was the first difficult decision my mom and I had to make about this new career of mine.

So we moved to New York and stayed with one of my mom's friends. We started shooting in the summer of 1984, so I didn't have to worry about school yet. But by the time our second episode aired, when we were working on our fourth show, the network ordered seven more episodes, bringing us to a total of thirteen. This pushed our shooting schedule right into the middle of the school year, and it meant I'd have to get my school in Los Angeles to set up a correspondence program for me to keep up; that didn't work out too well, because it wasn't something my school ever had to deal with before, and so by the second semester, after "The Cosby Show" finally got a season-long commitment from the network, I transferred to Professional Children's School in New York.

Professional Children's School, or PCS as it's called, is not anything like you'd expect. Sure, they've got proms and basketball teams and other extracurricular stuff the same as other schools, but everything is done on a pretty small scale. There were only about fifty kids in my graduating class. Most of my class work was done on "The Cosby Show" set, one-to-one in my dressing room with a tutor, during the in-between times in rehearsals. (No, I did not have to take classes with Keshia and Tempestt and Lisa.) The only time I ever actually went to classes at PCS was when we were on hiatus (that's television-speak for vacation), which amounted to about ten weeks or so during the school year. Believe me, it was a big adjustment from what I was used to.

There were other big adjustments too, right from the start. People began to recognize me on the street. Really, they'd flag me down and ask for autographs, and that took some getting used to. Also, I had a tough time making friends at first, because it seemed as if most kids wanted to be around me just because I was on a television show. That can get pretty weird. But I still tried to keep everything in perspective. I didn't let things get to my head the way I did when I got my first jobs on television. I was glad I got that swelled head phase out of my way when it didn't matter so much.

Now sometimes I wonder what my life would be like if "The Cosby Show" hadn't come along when it did. It's strange, because so much has happened in the past four years; it's almost as if I've had two different lives, my life before Cosby and my life since. If "The Cosby Show" never happened for me, I'd probably still be out in Los Angeles, getting ready for college, just like any other kid.

Probably I'd be playing some basketball, maybe working as a bag boy in a grocery store or something, still doing plays in that community theater. I don't know if I'd be thinking in terms of acting as a career, but I know I'd be keeping it up as a hobby.

Sometimes too I get to wondering what life will be like after Cosby. It's a scary thought. It'll all be over in a few years, and there are no guarantees that I'll keep working. This business is not promised to anyone. When you're younger, the pressures of acting are different from the pressures when you're an adult. Getting work doesn't have anything to do with putting food on the table or a roof over your head. That changes very quickly when you get to be my age. That's why school is so important. I know it sounds like a cliché, but I think you do need a solid foundation to fall back on. All the wonderful things that have come my way because of "The Cosby Show" can all disappear in an instant, and that's okay if that happens. I'm prepared for that. I've had a fast and wonderful ride, working at something I love, and I wouldn't trade it for anything.

Thanks for asking.

3

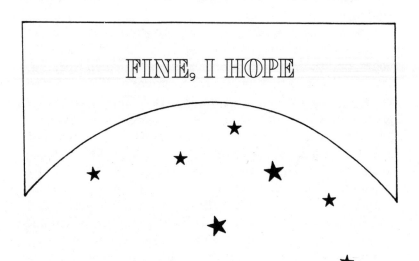

FINE, I HOPE

NOTES FROM THE LIGHTER SIDE

You are my eighteenth favorite star. Ahead of you is Lisa Bonet, Michael J. Fox, Michael Landon, Magic Johnson, Eric Dickerson, Pee Wee Herman, the guy from "Growing Pains," ALF, Christie Brinkley, Bill Cosby, Bruce Springsteen, and some others I can't remember.
—Aaron, 13

This may sound sort of personal, but how much do you get paid?
—Kirstina, 10

*My teacher has guaranteed that you will write
me back a letter by the end of the summer, and
we don't want to make a liar out of my teacher.
Do we?*

                                               —Breanna, 12

*I love your TV personality. I think you are a
radical dude.*

                                               —James, 11

I get some pretty funny fan mail, real day-brighteners.
Some of the stuff makes me laugh out loud, and some of
it makes me feel good, and some it just makes me scratch
my head and go, "Huh?" I'm dragging my feet here, I
know, getting to some of our more serious issues, but, like
Theo Huxtable, I'm a confirmed procrastinator in almost
everything I do. Writing a book is no different. Besides,
this book has got to be at least a little bit fun to read
(taking the pulse of America's young people shouldn't be
a tedious chore), and some of these offbeat letters will
lighten things up nicely. Think of this chapter as a spoon-
ful of sugar to help the medicine go down.

In case you were wondering, I take the heading for
this section from the way kids open more than half my
letters: "Fine, I hope." It's a line that follows the typical
opening question "How are you?" the way fries follow
cheeseburgers, the way D.M.C. follows Run, and it's almost always a signal to me that I'm in for a good time.

Oh, and I promise, I'll wipe this wide smile off my face
as soon as we get out of this chapter.

*Are we related? Your last name is also some-
where in my family, so you could be a long-
distance cousin or something.*

                                               —Rosanna, 14

Could you do something to let me know you got my letter. On the show, try to do this for me, wave or something, or say something about me because I never miss "The Cosby Show." That's my family show. Just say, "My friend Alan wrote me from Connecticut."
—*Alan, 11*

I will like you to send me four posters, twenty dollars and a small hair-dryer.
—*Lisa, 9*

Sometimes I'll get back from a long day at the studio, or I'll be having some crunch time in one of my courses at school, and there'll be a letter waiting from a fan that just catches me completely by surprise and chases away whatever worries or troubles I brought home with me. You'd be amazed at the healing benefits of a funny letter from an unknown friend.

These, then, are some of the fringe benefits of primetime television.

My Cabbage Patch Kid is named after you. Theo, not Malcolm. I hope you don't mind.
—*Melissa, 10*

I wrote Michael Jackson and he wrote back and you're not half as famous so I'm expecting you'll write back, okay?
—*Cody, 15*

Could you send me a letter or a picture or a button? Please? You are my favorite actress.
—*Kevin, 12*

Then there are times, a lot of times actually, when I'll hear from a real die-hard fan, someone who's never missed an episode of "The Cosby Show," someone who seems to know more about me than I know about myself, or at least more than I can ever remember about myself. I'm always baffled, and at the same time flattered, by the letters asking for things like my shoe size, or my zodiac sign, or what kind of contact lenses I wear, what I had for dinner two weeks ago Saturday. The kids who write to me generally have a serious fascination with the life I lead off-camera.

Whoever it was who said imitation is the sincerest form of flattery didn't get the kind of fan mail I sometimes get. As far as I'm concerned, asking deeply personal and sometimes trivial questions is the sincerest form of flattery.

Check it out.

> *If you have a fan club that's ten dollars or more, forget me being in it. If you have a fan club under ten dollars, or ten dollars, I'll be in it.*
>
> *—Randall, 10*

> *I practically know everything about you. Well, what they print. I wish I could get to know the real you. You won't believe this, but I think I am in love with you. I am obsessed with you and I want you to know, I always dreamed about writing, singing, acting, or being on "The Oprah Winfrey Show" so I could get to know the real you.*
>
> *—Saundra, 14*

> *I know only what TV and magazines say about you. I want to know everything. How tall are you? Do you like fish or liver?*
>
> *—Eileen, 16*

For the record, my favorite color is blue, my favorite number is 1,374, my favorite food is pizza, my favorite frozen food is also pizza, my favorite holiday is Halloween, my favorite rock group is in Bryce Canyon National Park in Utah, my favorite floor wax is Mop 'n' Glo, my favorite element is hydrogen. It used to be ytterbium but I could never remember how to spell it.

It's amazing, the things some kids want to know.
. . .

> *True that when you were thirteen you ate two whole pizzas for dinner? I heard this.*
> *—Mark, 11*

> *If you spill something on one of those sweaters or some other Cosby clothes do you have to pay for it or what? Or do you just keep it?*
> *—Lucinda, 14*

> *I've been to 27 different states, not counting the District of Columbia. I've been there too. And Hawaii. How many states have you been to? Which ones are you missing?*
> *—Allison, 13*

> *Which do you like better, songs or videos?*
> *—Jodi Ellen, 16*

Most of my letters come from young girls, by a margin of about five to one, and these are some of my favorites:

> *We don't know each other, but you've seen me once. You may not remember me, but I was the girl at the taping of "Hollywood Squares" at Radio City in November. I was the one with the big mouth that kept screaming your name out.*

A lot of girls were screaming your name out, so maybe I should tell you what I was wearing. I had on this white sweater with flowers on it, and I had dark curly hair with a red bow in it. I was holding up a sign that said, "Nikki from Long Island loves Malcolm!" I think you waved at me and smiled. At one time I was the only girl standing up, so if you were looking then I was probably the girl you saw. Remember?

—Nikki, 17

I once had a dream that I was gonna play your girlfriend on the show. Then about a week later they put some girl on there. I wanted to cry when I found out you guys had to kiss. I once went with a guy because he looked like you. I know it was wrong, but I liked you so much that I couldn't miss out on getting something that was almost a little bit you.

—Claudia, 15

I was looking in a magazine and I saw that you can be on "The Cosby Show" as your girlfriend if you win and tell why you love Malcolm in one hundred words or less. I almost died. If I could meet you I think I would have hard golden eggs.

—Elissa, 12

My older sister thinks you're cute. Her name is Betsy. But don't get your hopes up, she isn't so beautiful. Her nickname is Pimple Face.

—Sarah, 12

When I saw you kiss that girl the other night on the show, it seemed like it was me. I wish I was in her shoes, 'cause your lips look like I can fall in love. I need feelings of lips like yours against

mine. I hope I'm not scaring you, like that's all I want from you is your lips. I don't like you just because of your lips but because of you. But admit it, you do have nice lips.
—Christina, 16

I get a lot of letters like that. You know, real gushy love letters. I love it. I don't know that I'll ever get used to the fact that there are girls out there in some wonderful places I've never even heard of who get all warm over my lips. I mean, they're just lips. Most times the girls who write are sweet and sincere and full of innocence. You know, these letters are surprisingly wholesome; girls send pictures, but they don't send dirty pictures. They talk about spending time with me, but they don't talk dirty.

See for yourself.

In the Spring it is my birthday, and I have told my family that my only wish is to have you over for dinner and conversation. Don't worry, I have already discussed this with my mom, and she and the family have all agreed to chip in and pay for your plane ticket. Be sure to tell your mother that she can come too, but she would have to provide her own ticket of course, sorry to say. It's still cold here that time of year so be sure to dress warm.
—Lorraine, 14

I think you are smokin'. Do you catch my drift? I bet you are the smokinest boy in your school and all the girls must be always trying to rap to you. You are the smokinest boy on TV I've ever seen. You are smokin' like a cigarette.
—Tanya

Here is my offer: next time you are in Wisconsin it's my treat. We can go to the movies, or to dinner, or roller skating, and you can be my guest. The only thing is my friends will all be there and you have to tell them all you're in love with me and the only reason we don't go seriously is that you live so far away. Deal?
—Debbie, 15

The guys who write to me are usually less affectionate, at least toward me:

Have you ever wanted to date Lisa Bonet, and if you did how far did you and Lisa go? And did you ever think about dating Phylicia Rashād or is she just like a second mother to you?
—Jason, 15

I like your show. I don't watch it very much because I made a bet with my mom to not watch TV for a year for one hundred and fifty dollars. It ends on June the first.
—Dewey, 9

I hope you don't mind but I told this girl we were first cousins. I don't know if she's a really crazy screaming fan or anything, but I thought maybe it couldn't hurt my chances. After I said it though I remembered we were different colors, you and me. Oh well.
—Josh, 15

Did I mention that I think I'm possessed by Satan? Well, have a nice day.
—Freeman

Do you talk hoodlum? If you do, the next time I see you (like I've seen you before), I'm going to kick you in the neck and beat you with a chair. Hoodlum talk is ignorant.
—Gregory

I like the ostentatious clothes you wear.
—Wayman, 14

Have you ever been to Alaska? People think Alaska is nothing but dumb Eskimos that live in igloos. Well, it's exactly the opposite.
—Rickey, 13

Theo, please hurry and graduate from high school on "The Cosby Show" so you can get your own show on TV like Lisa Bonet.
—Charlie and Sam, 15 and 16

Most of all, the letters I get are spirited and from the heart, and all of them together give me a great sense of what's going on out there in the rest of the world. It's fair to say that I don't lead an entirely normal life for a teenager, but I come pretty close and these letters help to keep my sneaks on the ground.

And the best part is that they make me smile.

You know, Mr. Warner, maybe we can be pen pals. But, I know you have too many fans to worry about. Well, if you don't return my letter by February 10, 1987, I will write to Soleil Frye and then to Webster and after that maybe to Gary Coleman.
—Peter, 10

Listen to me, Malcolm, I'm not that big a fan of yours. A lot of times, with actors and other ce-

lebrities, it goes to your head that people care about you so much. I'm a take-it-or-leave-it kind of person. So, can I have your autograph?
—Sienna, 17

But enough of all this fun stuff. I've promised you we've got some serious business to take care of here and my word is my bond.

So, yo—let's do 'dis!

4

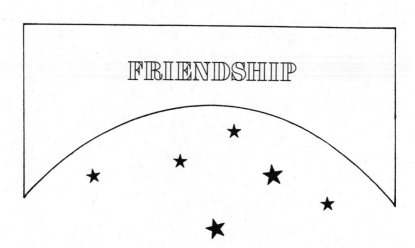

FRIENDSHIP

NOTES ON MAKING FRIENDS
AND FITTING IN

I think you're what I'm looking for. I'm looking for a friend. It seems like everything in my life is going wrong.

—Felice, 16

When I first saw you on TV I thought, I want a friend just like him, someone who I could always share my thoughts and innermost feelings with. Malcolm, to tell you the truth, I don't have many friends, and I feel very insecure about myself. The kids where I live are not very friendly. They don't think about anyone else but themselves. You are the only person besides God who can help me overcome my problem.

—Patricia, 16

Wouldn't it be great if everyone could just be themselves without worrying if it's cool or the in thing?

—Joby, 14

Most of the kids who write to me are looking for a friend. They don't always come right out and say it, but I have to think it's a big part of why they're writing in the first place. They'll almost always mention that they need someone to talk to, that the other kids in school don't understand them, that they've got something on their mind and no place else to put it. They're lonely. When a kid reaches out to me through the mail, when he really opens up, he is telling me that things aren't going as right for him as he would like.

Most of the kids I know are also looking for a friend. We don't always come out and say it, but we all are at least a little bit insecure about ourselves, about what our friends really think of us, about belonging to a group. Everyone is a little bit lonely, at least sometimes. I know I am. We all wonder how well liked we are, and even if we're well liked by enough of the right people.

Social life has a tremendous significance when you're in high school. It's way out of proportion. Every little thing —Am I wearing the right clothes? Am I too much of a know-it-all in class? Do I listen to the right music?—seems incredibly important. When you're in the middle of it, even the tiniest trauma, like having a pimple, can be a very big deal. Sometimes I think it's ridiculous, the way we put all this weight on the lightest things, but then other times I find myself falling into the same patterns along with everyone else.

Making good friends is not always easy, and it

becomes particularly hard when you add all the traumas and uncertainties of adolescence into the mix. But here's my theory: making good friends with Theo Huxtable is as easy as it gets. That's why he gets all these letters. He's one of the easiest friends a kid can have. Think about it. He's popular. He won't turn his back on you. You can hang out with him and his buddies, or with his family, on Thursday nights without worrying about what you look like, what he thinks of you, what your other friends think of you. You don't have to worry about saying anything stupid. There are a lot of things about Theo that make him a good friend—he's trusting, and loyal, and caring, and funny—but I think the thing that's most appealing to the kids who write is that he can't choose you or criticize you. He can't pass judgment. Theo Huxtable doesn't care if you've stayed home by yourself for the last seventeen Saturday nights, he doesn't care if nobody wants to go to the prom with you, he doesn't care if you didn't make the basketball team. The best thing is that he doesn't pressure you about drugs or sex or about doing things you don't feel comfortable doing, things you don't feel good about.

You can switch channels on Theo, but he's stuck with you, and that's an upper hand most kids will never have in their real-life friendships. What I'm getting at is that a whole lot of kids write to Theo Huxtable because he represents to them the kind of friend they wish they really had, or the kind of friend they wish they had a chance to be. And he's loyal, unconditionally so. He's always there. That's what goes into these letters.

> *I have never been part of the "in crowd." If you're not exactly like them, you are ignored. No one hangs around tomboys, that's probably the main reason I've never had any friends. I've tried acting like the other kids but it doesn't work. They already know what I'm like.*
> *—Pamela, 15*

So, when you're feeling in the slumps, if you feel like going off the Deep End, call up a not-so-popular friend: ME. A person who has real life problems. I am always ready to listen and I will try to help you solve your problems. We can exchange problems. You know, it's not good to hold all your worries and troubles in because you really get confused about life. So, if you want to come down to Earth, hey, talk to me. I'm really willing, and, most of all, trusting.
—Deborah, 16

I've been friends with this kid since kindergarten, and he's my best friend and everything, except he's become a real science geek and I'm still best friends with him and everything but I think some of the other kids don't like me because I'm best friends with him.
—Kevin, 14

Adolescence is a tricky time.

In every school, there's always an in crowd, and a not-so-in crowd, and an all-the-way-out-the-door crowd. That's a fact of growing up, and the thing that gets me is that no matter which crowd you run with there always seems to be another, better group which won't accept you. I guess the grass does always look greener on the other side, but there are things to be said for weeds. What I mean is, fitting in with the most popular group of kids shouldn't matter as much as it does. I know that it's easier to say that than to feel it, but it's something we should all keep in mind. If you're lucky enough to have a good group of friends, or even one good friend, you'd be smart to worry a little bit less about what everyone else thinks of you, and a little bit more about other, more important things.

If you have a good friend, it doesn't matter what

clique you fall into or where you're slotted in the minds of the other kids in school. Good friends are hard enough to come by; you shouldn't spoil the friendship with wondering how your friends make you look to everyone else. Kids like to form opinions about other kids without even getting to know them, and categorizing people by the type of friends they keep is one way to do that. There is a group mentality to growing up that can be very dangerous. Well, maybe dangerous is too strong a word, but things can get pretty unhealthy sometimes. It's been my personal experience that most kids are good and decent, but something happens to a kid when he's in a group that changes what's good and decent into something else.

A lot of these letters remind me how cruel some kids, in groups, can really be.

> *Lots of kids call me fatso and stuff because I'm overweight. I'm wondering if you could help and make me a little thinner like all my friends. I'm tired of being called names.*
> *—Marlene, 12*

> *Sometimes I get on the bus with the people that live near me and they pick on me. Almost every day I get off the bus and these kids call me names or say things about me. Sometimes they grab my shirt and pull it and stretch it out. My parents know but they say to ignore it.*
> *—James, 14*

> *One day there were these football players, they picked on me because I play soccer, and because I'm different. They make me feel like I don't have any friends, but the worst part is that it goes on everywhere.*
> *—Carlos, 15*

You wouldn't believe what happened to me today. I was at my locker, talking to this friend I sort of know from class, and a friend of hers comes up and invites her to this party on Friday. I'm standing right there and she doesn't even look at me, she doesn't even apologize for not inviting me. It's like I wasn't even there.

—Amy, 16

When I lived in Los Angeles, I had a friend who was always getting picked on. In fact, that's how we first became friends. We were in the seventh grade and he was the new kid in town, and everyone was giving him all kinds of grief, roughing him up, messing with him, but this kid just wouldn't back down. The other kids were really ragging on him, pushing him around, but I admired the way he wouldn't let them intimidate him, and I felt bad for him a little bit, so I stood up for him. I watched his back for him, and we became friends. When the other fellas saw that I was willing to defend him, they backed down. They left him alone.

I mention this story not to demonstrate what a nice guy I am, but to show you how easy it is to turn a negative into a positive. If you're like this new kid, the lesson is that you can't let people intimidate you into thinking you don't belong, or that you don't fit in. If you're the way I was, the lesson is that you can't sit idly by and watch your friends or classmates treat somebody else *like crap*. If you don't do anything about it, then you're as guilty as they are. And if you're like either one of us, the lesson is that it's sometimes easier to find a good friend than you'd think; you just have to know where to look.

I also mention it to show how big a role kids place on intimidating other kids. Fighting is a big part of growing up, at least for a guy. (After all, I can only speak from experience here.) Girls fight too. I see it all the time, and I guess it's not so different. Someone can start mouthing off at you and egging you on, and you have to do more than just sit there and take it. You have to do something about it. When you're older, I guess you can shrug off this kind of thing, but as a kid you can't turn away from it so easily. You're worried that if you back down the other kids will think you're a wimp for the rest of the school year. You may choose to ignore the guy who's picking a fight, but it's awful hard to ignore the way the other kids will see you as a result of your decision.

All the time I see guys get into such a big huff about such little things that it's almost funny. Things get heated and then they're letting off these huge amounts of steam, talking a good game, and at some point it seems that what they're arguing about becomes less important than beating each other up. It's happened to me a few times. I think it's happened to everyone. How many times have you been in the halls at school and seen two guys, or girls, drop their books in a huff, and start dancing around each other as if they're in a boxing ring? Maybe one guy will lunge at the other and they'll get into a clinch for a while, but eventually they'll break off and dance around some more. No one is really landing any blows. There's a lot of pushing and shoving, but no one is really hurting the other. They're just dancing around, saying things like "You gonna hit me? You gonna hit me?" until a teacher or some adult comes over to break things up. I don't think they always want to fight; it's just that they get themselves into these impossible situations where they at least have to go through the motions.

Fights like these are as much a part of growing up as homework. The way you handle yourself in them has a lot to do with the way you're treated by the rest of the kids in school. That's a shame, because the best way to handle them, more often than not, is to walk away from them. But most kids are afraid to walk away from a fight or a taunt because of what it may or may not say about them.

I live in an adult world at work and I live in a teenage

world the rest of the time, and because of that I realize there are things which aren't important in the adult world which are tremendously important to kids. When you're younger it's the whole thing about being cool, fitting in, not letting someone get to you. Appearances count. You're afraid to back down, and at the same time you're afraid to stand up. You're still shaping your identity, and if you don't fit in with the other kids they're telling you you've still got some shaping to do. That can be devastating to a kid. It means more, and hurts more, than it does later in life.

Later in life, if you don't hit it off with someone else, it's no big deal. We learn how to shrug things off as we grow up, how to balance what's really important with what used to be really important.

The other day I was in this fight with these other kids and I thought how it would be if you could come to where I live and be on my side in a fight. We'd take them, no problem.

—Matt, 15

My biggest problem is that I have trouble talking freely to others. For example, on holidays, when we go to see my relatives, I always thought I was supposed to be comfortable around them. But I'm just the opposite.

—Tatanya, 17

I am ten years old and in the fifth grade. I am not very popular in my class and I think that my classmates would love it if I came to school with your autograph. What do you say?

—Adam, 10

Everybody needs a friend. There's no getting around it. There's just too much to have to deal with all by yourself. In fact, I think we all need more than one person to lean on. I know that's true for me. I have different friends for different reasons, and I seek advice or comfort from different people for different problems. I have a lot of things going on in my life—acting, school, friends, family—and I can't go to the same one source for help or just for talk every time I'm confused.

There are certain things I'll go to my mom about, certain things I'll go to my dad about, but as I get older the list of things I don't want to talk to either of them about grows bigger and bigger. It's not so much that there are things I'm keeping from them, but I've got some things on my mind that they probably can't help me with. Well, maybe they can help me with them; it's just that I don't always want them to. When you're young, parents have all the answers, or at least they seem to, and that changes a little bit when you get older. Parents will still think they have all the answers, but they may not always be the best answers. Sometimes it seems that parents are too far removed from what we're going through to offer much more than blind support.

With guys there is sometimes a competitiveness in the air, particularly if the talk is about girls, and so if I'm having girl trouble I'll go to one of my good female friends and ask her to be my sounding board. But I can talk to my male friends about other things.

The point is you've got to have someone to talk to. If you have more than one person to talk to, that's gravy. But find that one person. You can't keep things all bunched up inside you. I tried that when I first moved to New York and I didn't know many people. There was a lot I would keep in. That was not the best time for me, and I'm glad I got past it quickly. When you swallow your emotions like that they can eat away at you.

Here's what I think. This school is a bunch of stuck-up jerks. My parents try to make me feel good and say the jerks don't know what they're.

★ 44 ★

missing, but it doesn't really bother me because most of them are not the kind of people I want for friends anyway.

—Rona, 16

Today in school I wore an earring through my nose, just to see what everyone would say.

—Sasha, 17

Hey, can I talk straight with you? Do you know anyone who is into material things as well as a show-off? Well, I do, and I don't like it at all. I have a friend who's into Gucci, Turkish ropes, Sergio Tachinni and all that stuff. This guy wanted to go with her and she said, give me something, and he bought her this white gold Turkish rope and then she dropped him. Can you believe it?

—Elena, 15

Do you have any regular friends? You know, kids your own age?

—Erica, 14

People ask me all the time if there are some things I've missed about growing up.

I like to think more about what "The Cosby Show" has added to my life than about what it might have taken away. The biggest thing is that it's made me much more confident and outgoing. I feel much better about myself now than I did before I started on the show. I wasn't exactly a shy kid when I was in junior high school, before "Cosby," but there wasn't much about me that separated me from everyone else either. I was just a part of the crowd. I had some friends, and we all thought we were pretty cool, but for all I know anybody looking at us could have thought we weren't cool at all.

But since "The Cosby Show" things are different. The best way I can describe it is that I'm on a different playing field than the other kids I know, than the kids who write to me. It's not better, or worse; it's just different, and it takes getting used to. My problems might be the same, I might be trying to play the same game, but the rules are changed for me. Or, at least, people don't expect me to play by the same rules. Now, I'm not complaining, because as I said I wouldn't trade what's happened with "Cosby" for anything, but I think it's important to try to explain here how things are different for me because of what I do for a living.

Things are different now because people expect certain things from me. They expect me to be like Theo Huxtable, which I'm not, or they expect me to open up to them and become best friends the first time we meet, which I can't do. When you're on a television show every week, there is something subtle at work which distances you from people, but at the same time there's something which brings you closer. This is a tough point to put across, so stay with me here. The thing is, people are afraid to get to know me even though a part of them feels that they already do. I come into their homes every week, and there is already a relationship in place by the time we meet, but it is a one-sided relationship. They already know me, or at least they think they already know me, but I'm meeting them for the first time.

Things are different now because I have to stop to think about why someone is interested in getting to know me. My exposure on the show has made me step out of myself and really look at who Malcolm-Jamal Warner is, and what he has to offer other people. Most of the friends I meet now I meet through my other friends. I am not in a traditional school setting, so it's hard to meet kids that way, and most of the people I work with are adults, or younger kids, and so I rely on friends of friends to meet new people. It's like that shampoo commercial, the one where she told two friends, and they told two friends, and they told two friends. After a while I've built this big network of friends of friends of friends. That works out great, because I'm meeting them knowing we're on some kind of common ground, but I regret not being able to go out and make some friends of my own the way I used to. I mean, of course, I can, except I'm never starting with a clean slate the way other kids are.

Things are different also because now I've got an image to worry about. Kids are always worrying about their image, that's true, but in my case it's a different story. I'm aware that Theo is a role model to a lot of young kids, particularly to a lot of young black kids. I accept that, and in a way I'm excited by it. Fortunately, I'm not a drug addict or an axe murderer or anything unseemly, so I don't have to change my life-style to be consistent with Theo's. Living up to his good name is a responsibility but it's not a burden.

I don't think I missed any great chunks of growing up because of "The Cosby Show." Maybe if I started on the show when I was five years old I'd feel different, but I was going on fourteen. I went to junior high school with the same kids I grew up with. I've had all the basic worries: Does she like me? Do I like her? Why can't I be more like this person or that person? I've been through that.

I still go through it to a certain degree. I still worry about what I'm going to do on the weekends, about how I'm going to fill my free time. I still worry if my friends like me, or why they like me. I still worry if I'll be invited to a certain party, or if my friends will remember my birthday. Sometimes I'm nervous about calling somebody up to go to a movie, or to hang out, whether it's a guy or a girl.

There are some things even "The Cosby Show" can't change. I thought that would be helpful for a lot of you to know.

5

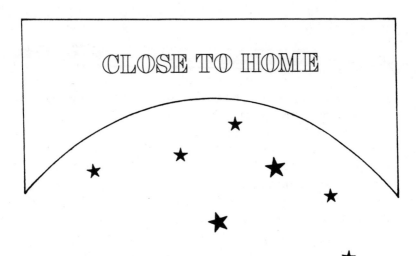

CLOSE TO HOME

NOTES ON FAMILY

After my parents got divorced, I think everyone gets along with each other a lot better.
—Melissa, 17

I feel sorry for you. You're always getting picked on. It must be hard to be the only boy.
—Kevin, 13

It's not fair what we have to go through with divorce. Listening to what mom says about dad, then what dad says about mom isn't fair. I'm always in the middle of everything.
—Rachel, 15

Sometimes I feel like my parents wish they had never adopted me. True. It's not my fault that I'm adopted, but someday maybe they'll just send me back.

—Rowena, 15

I wish my dad was more like Bill Cosby.
—Travis, 13

The thing I want most is to make my parents proud, yet all the time it's like they want better and better than I'm able to do.
—Marty, 15

Kids think about their families as much as or more than they think about their friends. I straddle the fence in both areas. I'm a friend to a lot of kids, but a lot of kids also think of me as a part of the family, or they think of themselves as a part of my television family. They see Theo Huxtable in his living room each week, and he's become as much a brother to them as he has a friend. And so I get as many letters about families as I do about friendship.

The kids who write see me as a big brother (to Vanessa and Rudy), as a younger brother (to Denise and Sondra), and as an only son in a family of four daughters. They also see me in "real life" as an only child whose parents are divorced, or as a stepbrother, from what they know about me off-camera. Their letters reflect my many different roles, particularly in relation to the letter writer's own role in his own family.

Sometimes the letters look at the relationships between brothers and sisters:

I don't know why I am writing this, but I know I have some problems but I don't know what to say. I guess me and my brother get into these fights sometimes. They have been real good. One

time we both had to go to the hospital for stitches.
                                        —Tito, 13

I have a sister who is 12 years old and even though she says she likes me I use her as my scapegoat. She is so easy to get to cry.
                                        —Robert, 15

It's like this: I have two little sisters and they're always starting fights with me. Personally I think they're very smart because they know if I hit them my mother will talk to me about it and she won't be polite, but if I tell her one of my sisters hit me she says things like, don't worry, you're bigger, they can't hurt you.
                                        —Lee, 14

And sometimes the letters look at the relationships with parents:

My mom and I fight. But we do love each other. We just don't get along.
                                        —Dolores, 16

One time my mother didn't like what I was wearing and she started fussing at me and she called me a tramp and some other names I won't go into. I mean, I love her and all, it's just that on certain days and certain times I really hate her.
                                        —Emily, 16

I get along with my dad pretty well, but he's out of town a lot. My mom and I just don't communicate well at all. It's bad. We'll get in a fight and she'll yell at me about how I do this and I

*do that and when I try to tell her how I feel she
cuts me off and I don't say it right.*
                                    —Joyce, 16

*My mom's always been nice and straight up
with me, but besides her I think I can't stand the
rest of my family. They never consider my feelings.*
                                    —James, 14

*My parents and I, we argue or disagree about
everything. We can't communicate. See, I believe in expressing my feelings and opinions,
and when I do that they think it's disrespectful.*
                                    —Angela, 17

You'd be surprised at how many letters I get from
kids who are unable to distinguish fact from fiction. I don't
mean this in any kind of negative way. I just think it's
interesting. Some of the kids who write get it into their
heads that I'm Theo Huxtable and they can't shake thinking that I actually live in a house in Brooklyn with Bill
Cosby and Phylicia Rashād and everyone else. They think
that's my real family. They think when the credits roll on
Thursday nights, we all go upstairs and take our turn in
the hall bathroom and then go to our rooms and turn in.

That tells us a little bit about the power of television,
but it also tells us a lot about how much some kids, and
some adults too, are willing to buy into a fantasy that is
much greater, or at least much easier, than their own
reality. Now, I'm sure on one level everyone knows we're
all a bunch of actors who get together each week to put
on a show, but on another a lot of people like to believe that
we really are a real-life family.

Take a look:

You really mean what you say when you talk to your sisters on TV, not like my brothers. My three brothers always beat me up and never take me anywhere. I wish you were my brother.
                                        —Lariette, 10

I like how your sisters are always picking on you. I have the same problem you do. My sister is always picking on me.
                                        —José, 11

I can't cope with the situation of having my room searched every time I'm not around. This is no way to treat a teenager. No way. A teenager's room should be private and personal, like your room is on "The Cosby Show." Does anyone go in there and search when you're not home?
                                        —Chuck, 17

I keep wishing Clair would adopt another girl on the show. I will be a great actor if she would adopt me. I live so far away but I could move up there. I could share the room with Rudy. I'm older but that's okay. I don't mind. Tell Clair to think it over about adopting me.
                                        —Marissa, 12

Well, I hate to shatter illusions, but I don't live in the house you see every Thursday night on television. If I did, I'd get pretty cold and wet sometimes. The rooms you see on the show have only three walls (the cameras and the studio audience go where the fourth wall would be), and they don't have ceilings (there are cameras, and microphones, up there too). There's no plumbing. And, if we're not using a particular room for a particular show, it's dismantled to make room for another set. Imagine that every time you left home, to go to school or to a friend's house or whatever, some construction people came and took your room apart, only to return and put it back together by the time you got back.

Let me introduce you to my real family. I live with my mother, Pam Warner. She's great. (I'll tell you more about her later on.) We live in Brooklyn, in a two-bedroom apartment where all the rooms have four walls and a ceiling and where the sinks and the bathrooms work just fine. There's me and my mom, that's all. My father, Robert Warner, Jr., lives in Chicago. He's great too. (I'll talk more about him as well.) He's remarried, and he lives with his wife, Carol, her son, Gabrae, their daughter, Collage, and my grandfather, Robert Warner, Sr. When I was growing up, before my mom and I left Los Angeles, I'd go to Chicago to visit my dad over the summers. Lately, though, because of "The Cosby Show," and because of other things, I don't have a lot of time to go for extended visits. We talk on the phone all the time, sometimes every other day, and even though we're not close geographically, we're very close emotionally.

So, like a lot of kids growing up today, I'm a child of divorced parents. That's something that can be awful tough on kids, but it's been okay with me because I never knew a different life, or a different way of being with my family. But, divorce or no divorce, I don't think of my family as "broken" in any way. It certainly doesn't need any fixing. As far back as I can remember, my parents were separated. When I was really little, right after I was born, we all lived in Jersey City, New Jersey. We didn't all live in the same house, but we all lived in the same town.

It's funny, but after a point, my mom decided she wanted to move back to California, where she was raised, and my dad decided he wanted to move back to Chicago, where he was raised. It's as if they tried to start a family on some neutral ground in New Jersey, and when it didn't work out there was no reason not to go back where they started. I went with my mom out to California.

I was about five years old when my parents finally got a divorce. I still remember very vividly talking to my dad on the phone when he called me up in California to tell me that he and my mom were getting a divorce. I said, "Oh, what's that?" because as far as I knew they were never really together. I don't remember ever asking why mommy and daddy didn't live together. I might have, I guess, but if I did, I don't remember. I always knew my mother loved me, and I always knew my father loved me. I felt loved by both of them. At five years old, with my dad already half a continent away, I didn't see how this thing he called divorce would change anything for me or for my family. I never knew enough to hope they would get back together; for me, they never really were together.

Well, my parents were together long enough to have me, but that's about it.

> *My parents are divorced, but my mother's remarried. My father and I talk to each other, but we don't have a steady, good relationship and I really hate it. Well, I have to live on. I understand your parents are divorced also. It's a terrible thing. Anyone hates to have to go through it, but sometimes there are no solutions.*
>
> —*David, 16*

> *I live with my father's mother. My father lives in San Diego, California. My stepmother, she lives in Miami Beach. My real mother is dead a long time. Well, you can say I am an only child, like you are. It's fun at times, being alone, then it's not.*
>
> —*Tamika, 15*

My dad is getting married. I hate the lady he is going to marry. I really don't like to say that, but I really think it is true. I have tried to talk to other people about it, but I really don't think they care. They are too involved with their boyfriends. I have a sister a year younger and a stepbrother and sister who are also a year apart. There are a lot of us.

—Chica, 14

Do you get along with your brothers and sisters? I get along with my real brother and my stepsister, but me and my half brother don't get along well.

—Beth, 14

When my parents split up, they still got along. They still do. That's probably the biggest reason why I don't feel the pain of their divorce the way I might, the way other kids feel the pain of their parents' splitting up. They're like a brother and a sister to each other. That's rare in a divorce (really, it's rare in most relationships, particularly among brothers and sisters), but it's helped us all to smooth out the rough spots in our whole family situation. I'm sure if they were arguing all the time—about money, about me, about whatever—I'd feel different about the whole thing.

But I'm lucky. Divorce, I'm told, doesn't always work this way.

I don't really like my stepfather too much, because he yells at me for things I didn't do, but I don't want my mother to get a divorce again. If she does then I'll have to move again and try to get along with a new stepfather. This one isn't so bad.

—Jason, 12

★ 55 ★

Of course, I don't know you or anything, so I don't know why I am spilling my guts to you. Well, my mother has been divorced twice and now she's dating with this guy who's like fifty years old. He's pretty big and he has a very bad temper and he hits my mom and it's not a normal hit. Thanks for listening.
—Emanuel, 14

Most of the time me and my stepfather get along, but when I do something wrong he gets mad. I mean, punching holes in the wall mad.
—Rosanne, 14

I have a feeling my parents are going to wind up getting divorced. They fight sometimes and when they fight I tell them, why are you doing this? Later on in the week my parents will get back together and be just as cute as a dove.
—Carlotta, 16

Dealing with stepfamilies can be hard. I know, I know, tell you something you didn't already know, right? But it is kind of weird how the Cinderella syndrome automatically comes into play after you get a stepparent. It happened to me, at least to a degree. Things got off to a pretty good start with my father and his new wife and their new situation. I was the best man at their wedding. How many kids get to be the best man at their father's wedding? I had a white suit on and a red shirt. I looked pretty cool. I knew what was going on. I knew my dad was getting married again to someone who wasn't my mom. My mom didn't go. She was back in California. But I made the trip and I stood up for my dad and things went okay for me. I mean, I was only seven years old.

It was after the wedding that things started to get strange. My dad's wife and I had some problems after they got married and throughout most of my growing up. Not big problems, but a lot of little problems that can end up being almost as painful. Before they got married we got along fine. It was just afterward when we both started to change. I think I resented her trying to be a mother to me. I'm not really sure what her problem was. I know the easy thing to do when a "blended" family isn't blending according to plan is to blame the kid for any problems, but I really think we both contributed to the cause. I want to believe things have gotten better now between me and my dad's wife because we've both gotten more mature, because we've finally gotten used to each other and to our new roles.

Now, I don't know if things would have been any easier, or more difficult, if I lived with my dad and his wife all the time. When I was there, in their house, I was always clearly visiting. I made myself at home, but I definitely felt like a guest. My father had this whole new family he'd made for himself, and I didn't really fit into it. I didn't think of it as my family; I thought of it as his family. It wasn't like "The Brady Bunch." (It's never like "The Brady Bunch," from what I hear.) I never thought of Carol as my stepmother, or as any kind of mother. She was my dad's wife. Chicago is where they live. It's not where I live. I have some friends there, from the summers and through Carol's son, Gabrae, but I didn't grow up with these kids.

When I'm there I'm always just passing through.

My parents are divorced and my dad is remarried. His new wife is sort of mean. My older brother hates her and doesn't try to hide his feelings.

—Michael, 14

I know how it is, living with one parent. My parents are divorced but my father still wants

*to come over to our house, but when my mother
lets him stay he tries to be with his girlfriend.*
—*Sloan, 16*

*My father thinks that my mother is having an
affair with somebody else. Once I was so sick of
hearing my parents argue that I held up a baseball bat in front of both of my parents, threatening to hit them if they started a fight.*
—*Lara, 17*

*Let me tell you about my stepmother. At first,
I thought she would be nice. But she's greedy. If
I asked her for a cookie she'd say no, but if her
son, my stepbrother, asked her for a cookie
she'd give him five.*
—*Christopher, 14*

And speaking of stepbrothers . . .

I've never thought of Carol's son Gabrae as a stepbrother, even though that's what we are to each other. As
long as my dad's been remarried, I've thought of Gabrae
as my brother. Now, we don't live under the same roof all
year long, the way other brothers do, but when we're
together we get along just like any other two brothers, and
when we're apart we think of each other just as any other
two brothers do.

It's nice, in a way, that I sort of inherited a brother like
Gabrae. We're only a year apart, and yet we don't have any
of the typical conflicts biological brothers have when
they're that close in age. We don't compete for our parents' attention, because we have different parents. We
don't compete among our peers, because for the most part
we have different friends. We don't even compete in the
classroom, or in the gym, because we go to different
schools.

Instead, what we do is hang out together. For most of the year, he goes his way and I go mine, but the few times we're together we just slip into this easy, natural way of being with each other. Relaxed, with none of this other baggage you get in some other stepfamilies. We've been thrown together by circumstance, but we happen to like a lot of the same things. Things are pretty cool between us.

Okay, again, I'm lucky. I've got a pretty nice relationship with my stepbrother. If you think that's special, wait until you hear about my sister Collage. Actually, she's my half sister, but I only make that distinction here, in print, to help you keep the relationships straight. I can't imagine loving her any more, even if we did share two parents instead of one. If I had to come up with one thing I regret about my success on "The Cosby Show," and what it does to my time, it's that I don't get to grow up with my little sister. Or, more correctly, that she doesn't get to grow up with me.

Collage is eight years old, and she's at that age where she always wants to hang around with me and my brother. Actually, she's always been at that age. That's okay, though, because I'm not there enough for her to get on my nerves. When I'm not there I worry about her, because things must be pretty hard to figure from her perspective. I mean, when I talk to my sister on the phone, she says things like "Hi, Malcolm, how's Rudy?" I'm pretty sure she doesn't think Rudy Huxtable is her sister too, but I honestly don't know what she thinks. She's growing up and she's seeing her brother on television, and I have a different name there and a different family. She sees me there more often than she does in "real life." I started on the show when she was only three years old, so probably that's as far back as she can remember about me.

Think about it. She knows we both have the same father, but then she sees we have two different mothers, and then on television I have four sisters and a brother-in-law and another father and another mother. I even have a different personality. I'd hate to be her shrink when she grows up. But seriously, it tears at me a little every time she says something like "How's Rudy?" Everyone else in my immediate and extended family has a pretty firm grip on reality, but for Collage reality is still taking shape. I hate it that what I do confuses her the way it does. I only hope that someday, when she's older, I'll be able to help her fit things together in a way that makes some sense.

My little sister really is a terrific little package. I wish I could be with her more often, for her sake and for mine. Okay, so I'm lucky again, right? I've heard stories, though, that would turn your stomach about how some kids get along with their stepsiblings and half siblings. Not only is life in a blended family not like "The Brady Bunch," it's not even close. Really, I don't know of any traditional nuclear family that gets along the way those Bradys do.

There are so many guys that can relate to you. You, being the only son in a family of all women, are in the same situation my brother is in. By watching you, his attitude has changed.
—Shalice, 14

Are you really the same way at your real home as you are on Cosby? I've seen your mother before on television, and I think you look similar to her. So, you still have to wash dishes, huh? Me, too! It's the pits!
—Darnell, 14

People ask me all the time what it's like to be an only child. To tell the truth, I kind of like it. I was never lonely when I was growing up, not that I can remember. I always had my toys—my Legos, my Star Wars action figures, my Matchbox cars, my jeeps and tents and campers—and I always had my stuffed animals, and it was always cool because when I played I never really had to worry about dealing with someone else. I never had to worry about someone else's input. I could play with my two figures over here, and then move over there and do something else, and I didn't have to deal with any conflict. Everything went the way I wanted it to go.

Also, I was able to fit myself into different roles. I could be a big brother to my little sister Collage, and then when I got tired of that I could go home. I could have my mother's full attention, or I could have my father's full attention. In school, I never had to follow in an older brother's or sister's footsteps, and either live up or live down to their name. And I've never had to play the doting big brother on any full-time basis.

Besides, I've always been around lots of kids. When I was growing up, my mother's friends all had kids my age. (They all happened to be girls, by the way.) There were kids around when I needed them. I was active after school in a whole lot of activities, like basketball and acting classes.

Sure, I suppose it might have been nice to have a brother or a sister around the house when I was growing up, but I guess I'll never really know what I might or might not have missed. Some of the kids who write to me, though, seem to make more of it than I do.

There are five in my family and I'm the second oldest. It's OK, I still have the responsibilities of being the oldest, but I always wonder how would it feel to be the only child. Maybe you've wanted another brother or sister when you were little.
—Patricia, 15

We both are only childs and I too live with just my mother. I wish we were friends so we could discuss how we feel about being only childs, be-

cause most of my friends come from big fami-
lies and don't know how it feels. They just think
it means being spoiled and getting everything
you want, when you and I both know that's not
all it means.
                                            —Nina, 17

We have a few things in common. Our birthday
is the same day but not the same year. I don't
have brothers or sisters. My mom and dad don't
live together.
                                         —Gordon, 14

Not all families are created equal. Well, strike that: they are all created equal; it's just that something happens in some families which changes the picture. I get a lot of letters from kids who are being abused and beaten, by their parents or by other members of their family. I don't mean to get into a complicated discussion here about abused kids, because I don't think this is the place for that kind of message, and I don't think I'm the appropriate messenger, but I feel I should at least say something about it to reflect what I see in the letters I get. You see, every so often, a letter will turn up that rips my heart out. Some of these kids go through a lot. I don't know what to do for them except to give them voice here. Maybe in hearing them other kids will know they're not alone, and that help is available.

I hope so.

My father abuses me. Still, after I told about it.
Let me tell you what he used to do, and still does
to me. He punches me in the face or he'll lock
me up in the bathroom from breakfast until
tomorrow.
                                         —Marcus, 13

It bothers me that my father would sexually abuse me and ever since he started doing it I think everybody hates me. Anybody who sexually abuses teenagers needs the rest of their life in prison. Sometimes I wish I wasn't born, because everything that happens I'm the one to blame for it.

—Stacy, 15

I have an imprint, literally, on the back of my thighs where my mother hit me with a wooden spoon she uses for cooking, and yet she asked me a few days later what it is from.

—Violet, 13

As long as we're on the subject, let me just slip in a note on family violence. If there's even a hint of it in your home, or in the home of a friend, get help. If you've read with me this far, you're smart enough to know what's right and what's not right in a relationship. Allowing yourself to be abused by a parent, or a sibling, or anyone else is not right. There are some telephone numbers at the end of the book you can call for help.

At home some kids get beat. It is a problem with my friend. At home her mother beats her if she's a minute late, or if she spills something.

—Glenda, 15

Here's the problem. My oldest brother is 24 and he's still at home and I think he is slow. My other brother is also at home and he doesn't have a job. A few months ago he beat me up. My sister, I found out, is bisexual. Her bisexual friends are always asking me to do things with them that I don't even want to talk about.

—Hallie, 14

I promised you a word or two about my mother.

She's something special. I know all kids feel that way about their own mothers, but I think my mom is especially special. It's not so easy being a single parent, particularly a single mother. She's done a terrific job (I don't mind saying); she's helped me to nurture this new career of mine without ever pushing me one way or the other; she's taught me all the differences, even the subtle ones, between right and wrong. She's helped me to shape myself into the kind of person I'm proud of being.

The best thing is she's a whole lot of fun to be around. All the rest would be worth squat if we didn't enjoy being with each other. That's key. Because it's just the two of us, and because we work together (she manages my career) and travel together, we spend a lot more time with each other than most mothers and sons. But it's not painful time. I think we both genuinely look forward to our times together.

Now, I'm not saying all this because I know she'll read it and I'll get into trouble if I am less than flattering. (That last part is probably true, but she also deserves every nice thing I can think to say about her.) I'm saying this because it's the least I can do. My mom doesn't need to pick up a book to read how I feel about her. She knows.

> *I saw you and the cast of "The Cosby Show" talking about your real parents. I really admire your mother. Her commitment to you, and your communicating with her. She is a wonderful mother. You're very lucky.*
> *—Tami, 15*

Tell me about it.

My dad's no slouch either. I don't feel cheated by not having him around. I don't feel jealous that he's living with this "other" family. He's always been there for me. There hasn't been a time yet, in all our years apart, when he

(RIGHT) My maternal grandparents, James and Thelma McGee.
(BELOW) Not quite one year old on Mother's Day, 1971. That's a picture of my namesake, Malcolm X, in the background.

(ABOVE) *My first birthday.*
(LEFT) *My paternal grandmother, Alpha Kate Warner, and me in Chicago.*

(ABOVE) *Having a good time at age three in Jersey City.*
(ABOVE RIGHT) *Five years old and proud of it.*
(RIGHT) *My kindergarten picture from Angelus Mesa Elementary School.*

(OPPOSITE) Having fun with my mom at Disneyland. Little did I know that one day I would be one of their spokespeople.
(TOP) My mom and me relaxing at Disneyland.
(BOTTOM) Here I am, starting first grade at Angelus Mesa Elementary School.

(LEFT) My thirteenth
birthday party.
(BELOW) Celebrating
the big thirteen with my
dad and my mom.
(OPPOSITE) This was the
head shot submitted for
"The Cosby Show"
audition, sixth-grade
picture.

MALCOLM WARNER

(ABOVE LEFT) *On vacation with Mom in San Francisco, 1983.*
(ABOVE) *This was taken on the ABC lot in L.A. during the last day of shooting for the "Cosby" pilot, 1984.*
(LEFT) *Mom helping me get ready for my first press conference, 1984.*

hasn't been there for me when I needed him. True, being there for someone over the telephone is a lot different from being there for someone in person, but I'd rather have what we have over the phone and over long distance than what some of my friends have with their dads under the same roof. If you have someone's head and heart, you don't always need to be in the same room with him.

Together, my mom and dad have worked overtime to build a nice life for me. Despite their problems staying married, and despite the difficult circumstances of my growing up, I think they've done a pretty terrific job of parenting. Of course, I guess I'm biased on this one, but that's the way I really feel. I'm sure there have been times when my teenaging stretched the limits of their patience, just as there have been times when they've gotten on my nerves, but I think we've all done all right by each other.

You know, when I think ahead to what my life will be like when I'm older, with my own family, I think of a nuclear family, all of us living under one roof. That's the way I picture it. I don't want to get married until I'm absolutely certain it will last and last and last. I'm not looking to rush into anything; that's why our divorce rate is sky-high. A lot of divorces are the result of marriages that were built without a solid foundation.

When I think ahead to the kind of parent I'll be, I know I'll be taking my cues from my folks. In fact, I'll pattern myself after them sooner than I will after the Huxtables. People ask me that all the time, if my real dad is like Bill Cosby, or if I'm going to be a father like Bill Cosby when I grow up. The answers are no and no. There are no real fathers like Cliff Huxtable, and there are no real mothers like Clair Huxtable. That's television. That's fantasy. I don't even know if Bill Cosby can be the kind of father Cliff Huxtable is, or if his family would even want him to be. But my folks are real and honest and caring and trusting. Better than that, they're my friends. That's so important. I want to be a friend to my children, and I want them to be a friend to me. I think it's ironic the way some parents expect respect from their kids when they themselves don't respect their children. There has to be a mutual respect there if the relationship is going to succeed.

My parents taught me that.

6

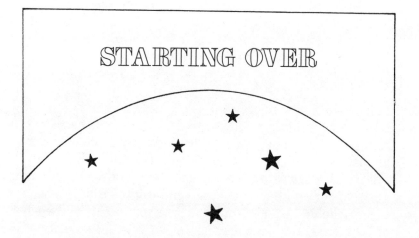

STARTING OVER

NOTES ON MOVING AND CHANGING
SCHOOLS

*I am at a new school now because my mom and
dad are divorced, see, and my mom said my dad
has responsibilities too, so she sent my sister
and I to live with him for a year and we're
moving back at the end of school. That's the way
she wants it, switching off from one year to the
next.*

—*Tracy, 15*

*Have you ever moved from one place to an-
other? Well, I have. I really thought my life was
gonna be great, since I was at a fresh start, but
it really isn't. Sometimes I cry at night 'cause*

I feel bad about the moving and wish I could move back where I used to live.
—*Pete, 17*

Here my father's got a worse job than where we used to live, and also we have to live in an apartment now instead of a house and I have to share a room with my two brothers. It sucks.
—*La Brea, 14*

Moving to a new town, or to a new school, can be one of the toughest things a kid has to do. Your whole world can change in just one stroke. The fact that it happens to almost every kid at least once doesn't make it any easier. Face it; it's hard to leave behind your entire world and start off for another, completely different world. It's hard to leave behind your friends and set about making a bunch of new ones. It's hard leaving the safety and security of the room and the house you grew up in. It's hard being the new kid. I'm sure there are things about moving which are hard for our parents, too, but it's also difficult for them to understand just how tough it can be for all the rest of us.

I guess one of the reasons moving is so tough is that the whole situation seems to the kid to be out of his control. The decision to go to a new school or to a new town, ninety-nine times out of a hundred, is made for him. I get a lot of letters from kids struggling to make new friends, to fit in, to bring a kind of sense to a time of disorder and confusion, and the common thread among them is that this is something their parents did to them. They blame their folks for the difficult times they're having.

Sometimes that blame is well placed and sometimes it's not. Sometimes parents have to move because of jobs, or their health, or other family reasons, but sometimes the move is motivated by the parents' simply wanting to offer the best to their children. Sometimes they take the long view of things while their kids are only thinking short-term. City parents may want their kids to grow up in the suburbs, or the other way around. Parents may come into some money and want to move their family into a better neighborhood, or they may fall on hard times and have to start over on a smaller scale.

I've had to move twice, from the East Coast to the West Coast and then back again. The first time, after my parents divorced, I was only five years old and nobody asked me what I thought about the whole deal. Nobody should have. I was much too young to contribute anything valuable to the decision-making process; I was so young that I don't remember much of what I was thinking and feeling at the time, and I tagged along without saying much of anything.

The thing I do remember about that time was going to my baby-sitter's house across the street from our new place out in Los Angeles. She had a son who was four years older than I was, which would have made him about nine. I have this very vivid memory of sitting with this kid in his room, and his pulling out this big hairy rubber spider to scare me. It worked. I was screaming my lungs out, and he backed me into a corner with it. For some reason the whole thing petrified me. I can still see the hairy black rubber legs on the thing dangling in front of my face.

Looking back, I sometimes wonder why that isolated incident has stayed with me more than anything else from that time, why I still think about it. Maybe it has something to do with how scared and uncertain I was feeling about this new start my mom and I were making in Los Angeles. Maybe it's because I was old enough to know that I wasn't on any kind of familiar ground but too young to know what that meant, or what it might mean. I don't know, but it seems to me a five-year-old kid can't really know that his whole world has been changed for him. But it's possible he can sense somehow that things are different, that things are happening to him and to his world that he has no control over. It's possible that's what I was going through.

Even at five years old, all the kids in my kindergarten class already knew each other. But at that age I don't remember feeling left out in any way. I was included right away; I made friends right away. I suppose what we can learn from that is that little kids are more accepting of change and new faces than older kids and adults.

Nice to know, right?

I live in Cincinnati now, a place that I don't like very much. You see, I used to live in Canton, that was up until February the 19th, 1985. That was the date I moved to Cincinnati. I love Canton very much. All my friends are there. When I moved here, I became a very sad person.
—Brook, 14

Just moved to this place in Maine. I don't even know how to spell the name of it yet. There's not much to do here. I've tried to make new friends, but that can get to be real hard. I've met some people that I really want to be friends with too. I told them all that I knew you. Look, Malcolm, it would really help a lot if you would write a few autographs and send them to me.
—Ross, 14

I have a problem with my new friends. At first when I moved here no one didn't even know I existed, and then they found out I have money, or my parents have money, and everyone wants to be my friend. Do you have this problem?
—Greg, 15

The second time we moved I was thirteen, and this time the decision was as much mine as it was anybody else's. As I said earlier, we made this move reluctantly, with only the promise of a six-episode "Cosby Show" commitment to go by. Maybe *reluctant* is too strong a word, but we were certainly hesitant. We weren't sure we were doing the right thing. Me and my mom were leaving a lot behind: she left her job, I left school, we both left our house and our friends. Neither of us was all that sure of our decision, I don't think, but we were able to ease into it by thinking if things didn't work out in New York we could always go back to California. We were able to tell ourselves we could change our minds.

When I first came to New York I spent a lot of time by myself. I had two cousins here, and I spent some of my time with them, but mostly I'd just be alone and listen to some music and think about my friends back in Los Angeles. I remember feeling that I was missing out, whenever I thought about what was going on back at school or with my friends. I felt there was this big party going on that I wasn't invited to. That's the way it seemed to me. I was lonely and I was bored. Eventually, I met some of my cousins' friends, and some of their friends became my friends by extension, but that took a while and even then I still didn't have any friends of my own.

I remember that as a very strange time for me. A lot was going on. On the one hand it was this tremendously exciting time for me and my mom—after all, I was going to be starting work as a regular on a network television show—but in the few weeks we were waiting to start shooting, I thought we had made a big and terrible mistake. I wished I was five years old all over again. Things were much easier then.

When we first moved here we were staying with a friend of my mother's in the Flatbush section of Brooklyn, and all the kids in our building or in our neighborhood would be out playing basketball all day. I'd hang around the park watching them play, not feeling a part of anything, and I was like that for a long time. Finally I got up the courage to ask if I could play, and they were like, sure, fine, come on. It was this big deal to me, their letting me play, but to them I was just another body on the court. Maybe they needed another guy to even up the sides. I don't know.

But the thing is that I got out there and I played, and after a while I became friends with some of the guys. I adopted this whole attitude on the court—you know, I was strutting around, pretending I was really Mr. Big Time—because I thought I had to do that. I thought, Here I am, a kid from L.A., playing ball in Brooklyn, New York. I thought I had to act the part, and I thought that's the way the part was played. I thought these guys might come on like that with me, so I wanted to have my guard up. I wanted to be ready.

After I was here a few weeks things were starting to look better and better, and I was able to let my guard down some, but I still missed my friends back home. I must have written my friends more during that time than I ever have since then, letter after letter after letter. I didn't call, because it wasn't our house and I didn't want to run up a huge bill, but I could have given our hosts a whole lot of housewarming gifts with the money I spent on stamps.

The letters kept up for a while, until I got busy with "The Cosby Show," and then they started to taper off some. I developed other interests here. I made new friends. Me and my mom started to build our lives all over again. We got our own place. We fell into a routine. My friends out in Los Angeles were still a part of me, but they were becoming less and less a part of me. It's not so easy keeping close when you're so far away, so some of my friends and I grew apart. They'd be gossiping about people I didn't know, and I'd be gossiping about people they didn't know, and in between we'd find we didn't have that much in common anymore. That happens, and it's not always the easiest thing in the world to accept. But I've kept up with a few good friends. Sometimes we won't hear from each other for six months or so, but when we do talk or write or meet, we just pick up where we left off.

There's this new kid in our school and people say his mother is in some trouble with the law which is why he lives with his aunt and uncle. I don't know what the story is with his father. He doesn't seem like a kid from a bad home.
                                                 —Sheida, 13

At my first school all my friends were rowdy and we would drink sometimes and get into trouble. That's just what we all did. But here for some reason, I don't know, the kids who are my friends are good students and they don't get into so much trouble. Funny, huh?
                                                    —Liz, 15

There was this girl in my other school, we hated each other and we were completely different and in different groups of kids and then I moved to this new school and the next year she moved to the same school. Pretty big coincidence. But now, get this, we're friends. Or at least we have the same friends. If you told me this would happen I would have said you should be in a straitjacket.
                                                —Dinitra, 15

Sometimes a change of scenery can be the best thing in the world for a kid. He probably won't know it at first, but he'll realize it later. I've had a lot of friends who've benefited from changing schools. Bad grades became good grades, bad kids became good kids, bad habits became good habits. Kids write to me all the time about the transformation they've seen in themselves, or in their friends, when they've gone to a new school. In New York City, kids change schools all the time; it's no big deal. In other parts of the country, though, changing schools is not always so easy; usually there's only one school in town and you're pretty much stuck there.

Moving was a good thing for me too, and I don't mean just because of what's happened with "The Cosby Show." In my case I don't think it had anything to do with changing schools, because I was doing well in school out in Los Angeles, but moving made me learn how to be more confident about myself, more outgoing. I had to put myself on the line more. It's a tough adjustment, but if you're going to get through it you have to put yourself out there. You have to be open and assertive and, in a sense, vulnerable. That's how you make new friends. A lot of that was made easier for me because of my role on "The Cosby Show," I'll admit it, but still it wasn't all that easy.

My feeling is that you've got to approach a thing like moving or changing schools with an open mind. You have to take it one step at a time. Sure, it will be rough going for a while, making new friends and finding your way around, but it's also a chance to do things differently, to start out with a clean slate, to try on new approaches to old problems.

The key, I think, to making a successful transition is not to rush yourself. Take things at a comfortable speed. Don't expect to be elected class president your first day in a new school. Keep in touch with your old friends—even make arrangements to go back and visit if it's possible— but try also to make new friends. Get involved with your new school, slowly at first, but get involved. Strike a balance between the old and the new until the new becomes less intimidating and the old becomes less familiar. You can cover up the rough spots by spending some more time with your family; if you've got brothers or sisters, hang out with them until you've got something else going.

I know. It's hard to be outgoing; it's hard to introduce yourself around to a group of kids who've known each other since their parents' Lamaze classes; but it's something you've got to do. I see some of this now, when I go to another school to take my Achievement tests, or my SATs. All the kids know each other, and I'm sitting in the back of the room, reading a book, listening to my Walkman, waiting for the test to start. I feel like an outsider. These kids have all grown up with each other, and I can't expect to be treated as one of them right from the start.

For me, now, because of my exposure on "The Cosby Show," it's a different ball game entirely. People think they know me, or they want to get to know me, or they have these preconceived notions about the kind of person I am. They expect me to be a certain way. In some respects, "Cosby" makes meeting new people easier, but it's more often the case that it makes things harder. I have to work to get past those preconceptions. Here's an example: One time I went to a basketball camp in Philadelphia with Bill Cosby's son Ennis. It was a two-week camp and we went for the second week, so everybody knew each other by the time we got there. We already had that working against us, but then we'd get out on the court to play and everybody would put on this attitude and say things like "I'm gonna stick Theo, man; I'm gonna stick him." Or, about Ennis: "I'm gonna stick Cosby's kid." They wanted to show us up on the court. We had to work extra hard to prove to these people that we could play ball before they'd take us seriously.

Nothing is ever easy, or at least it sometimes seems that way, but you can work at most things and overcome whatever it is about them that's difficult. That's the way it's always been with me whenever I've been in a new or unfamiliar situation.

Okay, it's like this. My father has this transfer he has to think about, and he asked us all to think about it too, but I've thought about it and I don't want to go. I don't care if it's a good job or more money or a bigger house or what. My friend Sandy says we should ask her parents if I can stay with them. No way am I going.
—Yvonne, 13

Today at school this girl came up to me and said, "You don't know what it's like around here." Then she said, "You don't know anything." Then she said she told all her friends not to like me because I'm new.
—Beth Ann, 11

I am writing this letter on how to be a good friend. I had the very best friend anyone could have. This ended the summer she moved. It was only about 20 minutes away, but since then we do not talk as much, she got on with the wrong crowd, she gets into trouble at her new school. We always thought we would be friends forever. I don't think that anymore.
—Maggie, 16

There's an old line that says you don't get a second chance to make a first impression, but when it comes to moving or switching schools that line goes right out the window. Really, it's one of the few times in life when you get a chance to make a second first impression. It's a chance to change some of the things you don't like about yourself and still keep the rest of you intact. It's a chance to make some new friends, and it's a chance to develop some new interests, and it's a chance to change some of the ways you interact with your family, and it's a chance to bring a new attitude to your schoolwork.

Moving to a new town or to a new school is tough, I know, and a lot is happening that's out of your control, but there are a lot of things about yourself and your situation that you can control. Turn over a few new leaves and make the best of what seems like a bad situation. It's a good idea to use the tough times to your advantage.

7

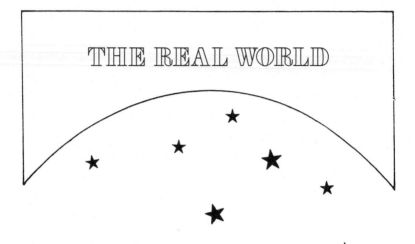

THE REAL WORLD

NOTES ON LIFE AFTER HOME
AND HIGH SCHOOL

Remember that episode where your family let Theo experience a taste of the real world? Well, that episode, it just stuck in my mind because it reminded me of my brother and how I thought he needed some of that same taste of the real world before he started college.

—Roberta, 14

That show you did makes the real world seem like a hard place to live. I don't know if it's for me.

—Kevin, 16

If it costs so much money to be graduated high school and living on your own like Bill Cosby said, then maybe I'll just flunk out and stay home. We've got cable.

—Blake, 14

The biggest response I've ever gotten from a single episode of "The Cosby Show" was from one called *The Real World*, which aired in our third season. It was all about how Theo decided he didn't want to go to college, and instead wanted to get a job as a model and set up his own apartment. He had a fantasy of what his life would be like and had enough of school and he was so excited about his plans he laid them out for his folks.

Well, as you can imagine, his parents were not at all thrilled with his thinking, particularly the part about his not going to college, and so they went into this elaborate detail to prove to Theo he'd have a tough time making ends meet without an education, and by the end of the half hour Theo came around to their way of thinking. It was one of the funniest shows we ever did, which is one of the reasons why I think it generated so much mail, but it also hit home for a lot of kids. I think that is the main reason I got the response that I did.

When it comes to providing for the big three—food, clothing, and shelter—kids, for the most part, have it pretty good, at least compared to the rest of the population. Sure, we've got to go to school, and we've got to help out around the house, but we don't have to worry about bills and we don't have to worry about taxes and we don't have to worry about putting food on the table. For a lot of kids, life is like living in a really nice hotel. If the plumbing goes haywire, somebody else takes care of it; if the stock market crashes we still have to do that paper on medieval history for our teacher in the next two weeks; if Uncle Sam comes knocking on our door for back taxes one afternoon, chances are pretty good we'll still wake up in our own bed the next morning.

Adult concerns are a real world removed from what kids are dealing with.

Of course, I'm well aware that some kids have it tougher than others, much tougher, but even in our lower-class and impoverished families the kids are protected at least to some degree from the nagging pressures and troubles of the real world, the adult world. I'm also aware that my real-world situation is different than most kids'. I've got a job, and I've started on a promising career path, and I'm making some important business decisions. In some ways I've already taken on a good deal of real-world responsibility, but in other ways I'm just as sheltered and protected as any other kid my age. I try to keep both parts of my life pretty separate because I don't want to cheat one for the sake of the other. It's hard sometimes, but it's worth the trouble.

All of us, I think, watch the clock until the big hand tells us we've hit eighteen years old, wondering what we're going to do with our lives when we grow up, wondering how and if we're going to get along on our own, wondering what our lives will be like in five years, or ten, or twenty, or fifty. Sometimes the clock seems to move too slowly, other times too fast, but always it's moving.

It's an exciting thing to wonder about, growing up and making a life on your own, but it's also a frightening thing to wonder about. That's what some of these letters seem to be getting at.

It's true, when you're at home and in high school it's like a cocoon. It feels like everything else goes on outside of where you are, like you're waiting for something to happen.
—Cheryl, 16

My brother can't keep a job, he's had five or six since he graduated, and he's saying all the time how lucky I am I'm still in school. He says I don't know what it's like because my parents still pay for me.
—Dexter, 15

I'm not like Theo. I work making deliveries for a drugstore after school, and on the weekends I have a business mowing lawns. My parents don't make me pay for food or anything, or rent, but sometimes I buy my own clothes, especially when it's things I don't really need.
—Thomas, 15

I'm not a money hungry person. I just want enough money to buy my family the things they've always dreamed of. My mother would like to own her own home because we have to rent a home because we have serious money problems. That's her dream. We're not poor, it's just that my father owes everyone.
—Millicent, 16

Let me tell you a little bit more about that *Real World* episode. It taught a nice lesson when it played on television, and it can teach a nice lesson here, in print.

The story went something like this: Theo came home after school one day and announced to everyone that he wasn't going to college, that he decided models make a lot of money and models didn't need to go to college, and that he had the right look and attitude to get a job modeling. He probably thought modeling was easy money, but for whatever reason he had his mind pretty much set on it. Cliff and Clair reacted so strongly because, in their minds, there was no way their son wasn't going to college. It was absolutely out of the question, as far as they were concerned. So they all had this big heated discussion, and when it was over Theo thought that would be pretty much the end of it.

What Theo didn't know was that his folks were just getting started. When he came home the next day the whole house had been changed on him. Cliff met him at the door and then gave him some Monopoly money (it's amazing, the mileage a show can get out of Monopoly money), and then pretended he wasn't his father, but instead was the landlord of a rooming house. He offered to rent Theo a room.

It took Theo a beat or two to catch on, but when he did, he was just playing along because he saw it all as a kind of game. He knew his parents were trying to teach him a lesson, but he went along with it to see how it would all turn out. So he said, sure, he wanted to rent a room, figuring the room he'd get would be his own room upstairs. He was only half right, because when he got upstairs he noticed all his furniture was gone. The room was bare: not a single piece of clothing or furniture, no stereo, nothing. Everything he'd need he was told he'd have to buy back from his mother, who pretended to run a secondhand store.

He was beginning to realize he was going to run out of Monopoly money sooner than he thought.

Eventually Rudy, Vanessa, and Denise got into the act because Theo had to apply for a loan (Rudy was the loan officer at the bank, and she turned him down), and then he had to go to a pretend modeling agency (run by Denise) to see about getting work. There he was told he'd have to put together a portfolio of pictures, which was going to cut into his budget even further, and even then there was no guarantee the agency could land him a pretend booking.

He was beginning to get the point. He was also beginning to get hungry, and the landlord told him he had to pay for his own food. His folks had set up the kitchen as this general store and restaurant, and Denise was in there charging him for everything he ate, even an apple. Every time Theo tried to get his family to break out of character and talk straight with him they pretended they didn't know what he was talking about. They pretended they'd never met him before.

The real world, Theo quickly learned, was a pretty cruel place.

In a way the show was an extension of the very first episode we did, the one I told you about earlier with the Monopoly money and the regular people. Then Theo was having trouble in school—he had just gotten a report card full of Ds—and he was telling his folks he didn't want to be a doctor or a lawyer like them when he grew up. He was prepared to take a less lucrative job—a "regular people" job—and survive on whatever he could earn. I remember when they asked him how he was going to pay for his food he said he could get by on just bologna and cereal. But this time, two years older, Theo was learning a different lesson. The first time he was being taught only the value of a dollar, but this time he was also being taught the value of responsibility.

Obviously, the lesson hit home for a lot of kids.

After we saw that show, my family did the same thing to my older sister, she needed to learn some things and she didn't see the show, only my father threw his back out moving her furniture out of her room. Her stuff was in the hall for like a week before he could move it back. She slept in my room and I don't think she learned anything from it.

—Lisa, 13

My brother pays all his money on computer games and CDs. He doesn't save. Me, I take my allowance and have it in the bank, and I have it in a money-market fund. I have a lot of money in there. All he has are a lot of computer games and CDs.

—Christie Sue, 15

What you should have done on that show was move into the basement. It would have been cheaper, much, and there was probably a cot you could use.

—Brian, 11

In my house we're already in the real world, believe me. Everything is on a point system and points are like money and if you don't do good in school or you don't clean your room or do your chores or whatever, you can lose points, and if you don't have enough points you have to do your own laundry or make your own dinner, things like that.

—Lizette, 15

Most of the letters mentioning that show do so only in passing, before going on to talk about other, related topics, but I'm interested in why they bring up the episode in the first place. I'm not exaggerating when I say that episode was mentioned in more of my letters than all of the other "Cosby Show" episodes combined.

Why?

I don't have a definite answer, but I do have some ideas. For one thing, the show opened a lot of eyes. It got kids to thinking that things will not always be the same for them as they are now. It's funny, most of the letters I got addressing this subject came from younger kids—up to junior high school age—and not from older teenagers. Maybe teenagers are already thinking about their approaching responsibility, and maybe they're frightened or at least intimidated about it. It's probably too close to reality for them to do much else than dread it, but maybe younger kids see adult responsibility as far enough away so that they can look forward to it.

For another thing, I think kids like to be told they still have a lot to learn, as long as they're not lectured about it. On the show, Theo learned for himself that he hadn't sufficiently thought through his plans on his own. Things were made clear to him by example. I don't think he would have come to the same realization if his parents sat him down and said, "No, you can't do this" and "No, you can't do that." Certainly he wouldn't have come to it so soon. His parents didn't lecture him, and I think kids like it when they're given a chance to make their own decisions, to draw their own conclusions. Kids responded to that, and in a lot of their letters they said they wished their own parents were more like Theo's.

Also, the *Real World* episode had a lot of "dress-up" in it. By that I mean that what Theo went through was not that much different from the way most little kids spend some time in their parents' closets, dressing up, assuming their parents' roles. It was fun for kids to imagine even for half an hour what it would be like to be in their parents' shoes, even if part of the fun was in knowing that at the end of half an hour they could go back to the way they were.

Of course, most kids don't do nearly enough to prepare themselves for the real world. Don't misunderstand me. I'm not letting parents off the hook here. A lot of parents don't do enough to make sure their kids are adequately prepared to leave the house and move out on their own. I see it even in the very simple things. I have a lot of friends who do not do dishes, who do not know how to wash or iron their own clothes, who do not know how to clean the house. They can't fix themselves anything in the kitchen except peanut butter and jelly and cold pizza. They have chores, some of them, but it's not the same as knowing what you're supposed to do to contribute to a functioning household, as doing it without being told. I mean, this is stuff I've been doing since I was seven years old. I'm not saying that the way I've been raised to be responsible and helpful around the house is *the* right way to raise a kid, but I'm prepared for living on my own in a way a lot of kids are not. I'm glad about that.

I also have a lot of friends who expect everything to be handed to them. They want a new pair of sneakers, or a stereo, or even a car, and they think they can just go and ask their parents for it. A lot of times, they're right. They can. It's like room service in that hotel I was talking about, and somebody else is picking up the tab.

I think something means more to you if you have to work for it. And it will mean more later, when hand-outs are not so easy to come by. If you want something, work toward it. I know a lot of parents who tell their kids if they earn half the money they need for something—a new dress, or a new guitar—they'll match it. That's a great way to give kids an incentive and some responsibility, and at the same time parents can delegate and encourage that responsibility.

It's important for kids to have goals, but it's important that they be realistic goals. To set those goals it's important to understand, or at least try to understand, what the real world is like. Ask your folks how much it costs to live where you live. Find out what your rent is, or your mortgage; find out how much your folks pay for food, and for clothes and for everything else. Find out how much it costs to run the air conditioner in your room for a month, and then see if that's a luxury you would treat yourself to if the money were coming out of your own pocket.

If you're already interested in a particular career, you can call up any appropriate trade organization—a hospital worker's union, if you want to be a nurse or medical assistant; The Writer's Guild, if you want to be a writer; your state bar association if you want to be a lawyer—and find out what entry-level salaries you can expect, how far you can expect to go (and how fast you can expect to get there). Find out how much it costs to go to the college of your choice, or to graduate school. Be realistic about things and figure out right now if your career goals will let you live the life and life-style you're looking for. The key is to learn to be realistic.

Parents, if your kids are old enough to understand and to be discreet, sit them down and tell them how much money you make and where it all goes. Teach them about paying taxes and about balancing a checkbook. If you have investments, tell your kids about them. If you have money put away for their college education, tell them about that too. Teach them how to plan a budget. No matter what kind of home you live in—a small, cold apartment or a big, comfortable mansion—there will be money coming in and money going out. There will be some kind of budget in place, and if the kids are involved, or at least aware of the family's budget, then they'll be a step ahead when it comes time to live with one of their own.

Dorothy was onto something when she woke up from her dream in *The Wizard of Oz* to discover there was no place like home. But that's Hollywood. All she had to do to make things right was click her heels and mumble. In the real world people grow up, and then there's no place like a home of their own, with a new family of their own, and when things go wrong it takes a lot more than wishful thinking and fancy footwork to set them right, no matter what kind of shoes you're wearing.

That's the lesson Theo learned on his trip to the real world, and it's a lesson I think a lot of kids learned along with him.

8

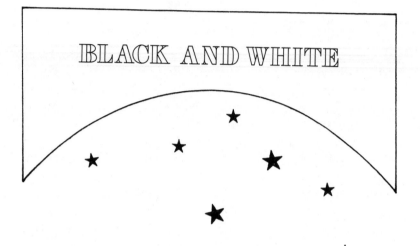

BLACK AND WHITE

NOTES ON RACE RELATIONS

It bothers me that the color of one's skin is ruling over our world. You never know how a person is until you get to know them.
                                    —*Frieda, 19*

I have light brown-colored skin, but I was adopted and my parents are white. All my friends are white, which doesn't matter to me. I think it matters to them.

                                    —*Ava, 12*

The school I go to now is full of mostly white kids. I'm not prejudiced or nothing, but there are only about 12 black kids out of 500 some white kids. The kids there are really prejudiced, so I don't have any friends. I don't have any friends to tell how I feel.

—Nadia

I'm white, but who cares?

—Bob, 10

If my mail is any barometer, kids today are as confused about issues of race and prejudice as anybody else. In a noticeable number of letters, the kids who write to me make some kind of big deal about the color of their skin. They bring it up, more often than not. I'm not saying I don't know why color is so important to so many people, but I don't understand why it should matter to a kid what color he is when he sits down to write me a letter.

A lot of times, it's the first thing they tell me. Sometimes it seems that if a white kid is writing to me, he's almost apologizing for being white; he's saying, "Hey, I'm white, but I'm still cool." If a black kid writes to me he's telling me, "Hey, I'm down with you; it's me and you." Both ways, it's as if they're looking for my approval, my acceptance of them, and the only way they can think to gain it, or at least the easiest way they can think to gain it, is through color. Both ways it says to me kids get all kinds of mixed messages when it comes to race and race relations; I'm surprised anyone knows what to think anymore.

The distinction between black and white is made, in one way or another, in most of the letters I get, no matter who's writing and no matter what the main point of the letter, and the overall effect is to leave me thinking that race relations haven't really progressed very far at all. Even the black kids who write to me insist on telling me just how black they are—light-skinned, chestnut, mahogany, chocolate, mocha—which reinforces the notion

★ 89 ★

that there's an even further prejudice within the black community itself. Sometimes I wonder how different my mail would be if I were white; I wonder if the issue of race would ever come up at all. I'm willing to bet that it wouldn't.

The fact is, I think it's impossible to grow up black in today's society without a very keen awareness of black history—of the injustices done to black people in the recent and distant past, of the prejudices that still exist today, of the civil rights movement, of apartheid. Growing up white is something different. If you're white, it's possible not to give race relations and prejudice a second thought—you can grow up with white friends and black friends and for the most part not notice the difference. If you're black, it's part of your heritage and it's part of the baggage you carry with you every day. It's drilled into you by osmosis that you're different. It's something you have to deal with. I don't know, maybe that explains why black kids want to let me know they're black, but I still can't figure out why a white kid would write to me and go out of his way to let me know what color he is, or why a black kid would insist on telling me exactly how black he is.

It all shouldn't matter as much as it does.

What I'm seeing in these letters is a subtle kind of racism, but it is a kind of racism. A distinction is being made on the basis of color, and certain preconceptions are being formed also on that basis. Either the kid doesn't want me to form any preconceptions about him, or he wants to let me know he hasn't formed any about me.

Away from the letters, I also see a subtle kind of racism among the people who know me from television. Here's an example: When I'm stopped for an autograph, people have certain expectations about how I should behave according to the color of my skin or theirs. I have a standard policy, when I'm out in public, that I don't sign autographs, because if I sign one I'll have to sign one for everyone else who asks. I don't mean to be a snob or anything, but sometimes I'd never get to where I'm going. I'm always flattered that people ask (I think I'll always get a special thrill out of it), and I'm polite as I can be, but I always try to keep moving. It's happened to me that I've been stopped for hours, and then when I finally did have to move on, there were always some people who were left out. I feel terrible then, but at least I have to try to get where I'm going. Sometimes the people who are left out say something nasty to me, or they're upset, and what could have been a nice encounter turns into something else.

Anyway, sometimes I'll be asked by a black person for my autograph and I'll have to use my standard line, and then they'll get all huffy and say something like "All right, be like that man! You're gonna be a star; you're gonna forget your people." Either they think I'm a sellout, or that if they wait around long enough for all the white people in the crowd to disperse, then I'll sign an autograph for them —that I'll treat them differently because they're black. It's ridiculous. One time I was in the mall over at South Street Seaport here in New York and this black woman, one of the security officers there, came over with a pen and paper and I told her, "I'm sorry but I can't sign for you." So she leaned over and whispered, "Come on, brother, do me a solid!"

Of course, more aggressive forms of racism still exist in this world, and they find their extensions in our young people. I get letters about this too:

One time in my school we had this thing where we would throw rocks at the white kids when they were waiting for the bus. Not rocks like stones or anything, but rocks like pebbles. You know, small. I did it because my friends did it, and because why not, but then someone took me

and they told me why was I doing it and I told them why and they said that's one of the dumbest things they ever heard.
                                                    —Carl, 15

In New York, where I'm from, we have this place called Howard Beach and there are problems there. Big problems. You know, problems with blacks and whites. People are fighting with each other for no reason except because they're black or they're white. Killing too.
                                                    —Clinton, 14

The Howard Beach incident has been in the headlines since December 1986, when a group of white teenagers got into what started out as a shouting confrontation at a pizzeria with three black men. According to the story as it was reported in the papers, the two groups tossed racial slurs back and forth until one of the white kids pulled a knife, and the three black men fled. One of the blacks escaped unharmed, another was reportedly beaten with a baseball bat and another blunt object, and the third was chased onto a busy highway, where he was struck and killed by a passing car.

For those of you who live in New York, or who read the New York papers, I don't have to describe the kind of racial heat generated by the incident and resulting trial. This was front-page news. (As I was preparing to write this, three white kids were found guilty of manslaughter and lesser charges, and a fourth was acquitted of all charges.) For a time there you couldn't turn on the news without hearing something about the Howard Beach incident, and everybody was talking about racial tension in the city.

When the jury came in with its verdict, after a long deliberation, there were all these marches and protests; the black community thought the jury was too lenient, and the white community thought the jury was too harsh. After the trial, there were reports of white kids' harassing blacks, or black kids' harassing whites, all the time shouting things like "Remember Howard Beach!"

It got pretty out of control, but I think a lot of the heated emotions were fed by the coverage in the newspapers and on television; a single incident became something much bigger because of what it represented, not because of what actually happened.

It's strange, but for all the media attention surrounding the incident, very little racial tension filtered down among my group of friends. My white friends didn't take anything out on me, and I didn't take anything out on them. Nothing was changed between us. We hardly even talked about it. We had other things on our minds, and right or wrong the incident at Howard Beach was not on the top of our list.

In a way it was as if it was happening to some other group of people.

You saw this Howard Beach deal, right? Stupid, huh? People should just be people and not care what color they are. Fighting is okay if it's for a reason, but what color you are is not a reason. I'm white (not that it matters, but just so you know), and I wouldn't pick a fight with a black kid for no reason. I mean, I would fight with him, if I had a reason, but I wouldn't fight with him just because he was black. This is nothing against you, but do you know what I mean?
—Peter, 16

I'm in a group of kids and we have this system set up where if we get dirt from the white kids we give them dirt back. It's a punishment system.
—Wanda, 14

There are these black kids in my school and sometimes before Homeroom we hide out in the bushes and jump them when they go past. They do it to us, right?

                                          —*Ritchie, 15*

Now, the Howard Beach incident and others like it show us racism at its ugliest, at its most extreme. It's prettied-up in most of the mail that I get, and in the attitudes I see at school and with my friends, but it's all a part of the same package.

I can remember when I was in the fifth grade, my school entered into an exchange with another school in a predominantly white community. I went to a school called Coliseum Street School, which was in my old neighborhood out in Los Angeles, and the school and the neighborhood both had a basically black and Oriental population. And then there was Marquez Street School, which was in a white neighborhood in The Palisades. Half of the kids from Coliseum went to Marquez, and half of the kids from Marquez went to Coliseum, and then at the end of each semester, we all switched. I was in the first group to go to Marquez and the people in the neighborhood seemed to be thinking, "Oh, my goodness, black people!" I don't know, maybe they thought their property values would plummet with all of us black kids around. That was one of the first times I can remember being on the receiving end of any kind of racial remark; before that I was mostly always around blacks, but I was also never in any kind of situation where I was seen as a threat because of the color of my skin.

It turned out that that exchange was a pretty positive experience. I made some good friends and we were all able to begin to break down some barriers. Well, maybe we didn't break them down so much as we started to chisel away at them. If I was with a friend, and that friend happened to be white, it was very clear to both of us that we were separate, different. It was an issue. It may have been an unspoken issue, but it was still an issue. It was a part of our friendship, even if we didn't think about it consciously. Cliques still tended to be all-black or all-white, but there were always exceptions, and I think the longer the program went on the more exceptions you'd find.

We are still a long way from any genuine kind of racial equality. I'm lucky enough to have some kind of success as an actor, and so I see less and less prejudice directed toward me from one day to the next. But it's still there. Oh, is it still there. As a matter of fact, now that I'm out there and working and meeting new people, prejudice has plenty of chance to rear its ugly head, even if people seem to separate me, as a celebrity, from any thoughts of racial equality.

Here's an example. When I started out on "The Cosby Show," before people recognized me, I'd get funny looks when I was flying in first class, or when I was checking in to a fancy hotel, or eating in a nice restaurant. My mom, who travels with me, still gets those funny looks. If we're flying first class, especially if she's flying without me, the other passengers will give her these double- and triple-takes, and eventually the stewardess will come over and ask to see her ticket to make sure she's not stowing away in high style. They don't bother with me because they see me as a celebrity, and for some reason that makes it all right. But with my mom, there's an attitude that suggests she shouldn't be up there with everybody else, with the white people. It's like the modern-day equivalent of the back of the bus—some people still think that's where we belong—and I always think to myself we've been through this; we should be past that stage already. But then I remember that the heart of the civil rights movement was only twenty years ago. It takes a long time to change.

Of course the best way to bring about that change is

through education, and the best place to start is in our schools. I think that if other school districts start more programs like the Coliseum-Marquez program, at the elementary school level, that might help to erase the perceived color line. We're probably a long way from that possibility in many communities, but it is something to strive for.

Know what? About three months ago I did a totally spur-of-the-moment thing. I applied to some private schools in Connecticut and Massachusetts. I don't even have the slightest idea if I'll even get in. The town I live in is pretty small and is very set in its way and has limiting ideas. I'm not ugly, not to sound like a "bitch" or anything, but in the ten years here I've never had a real boyfriend. The girls don't care what color you are, but the guys wouldn't dream of going with a black girl. The only other black boy at my high school is my cousin. (Great!) I just need a change of attitudes. Are they old-fashioned, or what?

—Linda, 14

I have nothing against black people because I am good friends with a black girl named Sherrell. So I hope you don't have anything against me.

—Lisa, 12

I'm not black and I don't think people should talk bad about blacks.

—Leah, 10

I think black people are really nice. My old boyfriend is black. Now my best friend is going with him.

—Josephine

★ 96 ★

I get a fair amount of letters on interracial dating and that surprises me. From what I've seen among my friends, and at school, interracial couples are rare among teenagers. Judging from my mail they're not all that common among the rest of the country, even though the subject does come up every now and then. It's interesting, but you'll see black and Oriental couples, white and Oriental couples, black and Puerto Rican couples, white and Puerto Rican couples, before you'll see a black and white couple in high school. This I can't explain, but if you ask any kid, at least in New York or Los Angeles, he'll tell you the same thing.

I've never been involved in a serious relationship with a white girl, but I did come close. There was this girl once. She was absolutely stunning to look at—her father was white and her mother was Oriental—and we dated a couple of times. The relationship never really went anywhere, and the issue of race never really came up between us. Looking back, it seems kind of unusual that we didn't talk about our very obvious differences. At the time, part of me didn't even pay any attention to what color she was; it was beside the point. But there was another part of me that was always waiting for something to happen; I'd be waiting for her to say something, and for all I know she'd be waiting for me to say something, and nothing ever got said.

There's an interesting story that goes with that girl. One time I asked if I could bring her onto "The Cosby Show" set as an extra for the show—she's a model—and I was talking her up and talking her up, and I told my buddies on the set how amazing-looking she was, like "Oh, you guys have to see this girl!" So I created this big build-up, and the next day she comes in and people were coming over to me saying, "How come you didn't tell us she wasn't black?" Now what is that supposed to mean? It's interesting to me the way these guys naturally assumed if I was attracted to someone she had to be black. If you ask me, the fact that this girl was gorgeous was the issue; the fact that she was white (technically Eurasian) was irrelevant.

To be fair, the fact that she was white is not entirely irrelevant; certainly the color of her skin would not be lost on my family. My uncle was very active in the civil rights movement, and when I was younger he used to joke that if I married a white girl he wouldn't come to my wedding. He was always joking, but now that I think about it he was probably trying to teach me to be proud of who I am, to be proud of being black, and that if you marry outside your race you are also denying a little bit of who you are.

But he was also teaching a kind of prejudice. His attitudes have changed a little bit over the years; he wouldn't say anything if I called him up and told him I was dating a white girl, or if he read about it in the papers. On some level it would probably bother him, but not enough that he'd interfere. My parents would probably be the same way about it. On some level, they would care, but on another it wouldn't matter at all. I did tell them about this girl, and they didn't seem upset about it one way or the other.

> *I absolutely adore your television program. You are my idol and I've always, always wanted to be just like you. I mean, just because you're black and I'm white doesn't mean anything at all.*
>
> *—Neal, 14*

At "The Cosby Show" we get a lot of mail, and we generate a lot of commentary, about how we portray a black family on television. A lot of it is positive, but I'm surprised at how much of it is negative. All the time, we hear that we're presenting a false reality to black people, that no black family can afford to live the way the Huxtables do. That statement in itself is derogatory. Underneath it people are saying that no black people in the United States are upper middle class, that there are no two-career professional black couples, that no black people have that kind of stable, loving family relationship to build on.

That's an insult to black people all across the country. And, worse, the unspoken message is not just that black people don't live the way the Huxtables do but that black people can't live that way. Or shouldn't.

Things got so bad that when Flip Wilson came out with his own family situation comedy a few years ago—maybe you remember; it was one of the so-called Cosby clones a year or two after we came on the air—it was promoted as the black version of "The Cosby Show." Now, that's sad. Flip Wilson was out there giving interviews and saying it himself, and yet on his show he played a character who wasn't as successful as Cliff Huxtable, who was married to a woman who wasn't as successful as Clair Huxtable, and who lived in a house and in a neighborhood that weren't as nice as the Huxtables'. The only real difference was in the life-style, in the measure of material success, and the network sold the show in such a way that it reinforced the same stereotypes people accuse "The Cosby Show" of ignoring.

The public relations and media people that surround the television business are also guilty of driving home a certain image of blacks. I picked up one of those teen magazines the other day and it said something to the effect that Michael J. Fox and Kirk Cameron are soon going to have competition in the heartthrob department because Malcolm-Jamal Warner is coming up. Okay, I can understand why they put Michael J. Fox up there. But Kirk Cameron?

Don't get me wrong, this is nothing against Kirk. He's a terrific actor and he makes me laugh. But "The Cosby Show" has been on longer than "Growing Pains," it's more successful than "Growing Pains," I have been out there a whole lot longer than he has, but they're still going to pump him up and play me down. That's got to be a racial thing, at least in some part. I can't understand it any other way.

Sure, if the magazine sends their photographers out with Kirk Cameron on a stroll through a white neighborhood, there is going to be a crowd of screaming girls to go, "Oh, Kirk!" But take him up to Harlem? Please. There will be a significant difference. You can take me through a black neighborhood or a white neighborhood and the reaction is pretty much the same, and yet the magazines and the public relations people don't pay attention to that. I get the same response across the board, black and white and everyone else in between; and the response to Kirk is more one-sided, and yet they make me sound like an upstart and make him sound like an established superstar. Give me a break!

In the heartthrob department, I even get letters from girls saying things like "I think you're cute, even though you're black" or "I know you're black but I still like you anyway." It's as if they have to qualify it if they have a crush on me, and I have to believe that kind of thinking reflects the attitudes of the folks who promote the show.

> *In my room, on my wall, I have 27 pictures of you from magazines and posters. My father says why don't you put up pictures of a movie star who is white for a change, but I say no way.*
> *—Christine, 12*

> *My father is a trial attorney and my mother is an architect and my sisters are all at college and I'm an honor student in high school. What do you think, are we white or black? Well, we're black, and it makes me mad what people say about your show.*
> *—Denise, 16*

I don't care what everybody else says, I think we're breaking new ground on "The Cosby Show." I think we're doing good things. I like it that I'm able to demonstrate a positive role model to other kids, black and white both, but black kids in particular. Theo Huxtable is the first black kid on a weekly television series who does not live in the projects, who is not a hoodlum, who does not have a midget brother, and who does not have white parents. That's a big thing.

I like it also that I work on a show that fosters the values of a strong, loving family relationship: one that sends the right signals to viewers that your life-style doesn't have to have anything to do with the color of your skin. That's a big thing too.

As an actor, I worry if I'll always be so lucky. Already I see a certain stereotyping in the roles I'm offered outside "Cosby." They want me to play a street kid, or a punk, or a token black; nobody sends me scripts which make no mention of the race of the character I'm supposed to play. Lately, I'm thinking that if there are no roles out there I want to play, I'll have to go and write them myself. Or at least find properties with positive roles for young black actors and produce them. You don't see many black people behind the camera, in positions of power, in this business. That's where I want to be.

There's a cycle at work here, and sometimes it seems it will be hard to break. Black people don't get the strong roles on camera because there aren't enough of us working in this business behind the camera. But how are we going to get more people behind the camera—writing, producing, directing, editing—if they're not excited about what they're seeing on screen?

We have these set notions that black people can do this and white people can do that and the television shows and the movies we watch reinforce those notions; I think by getting in a position to make new choices I can break away at that. You have to educate people: you can't just expect them not to think in terms of black and white all of a sudden. It has to happen slowly. But then again you can't just sit down and talk about it. It takes more than theory to shake loose our set notions, and I think by writing and producing and directing I can turn that theory into action. I want to get out there and I want to do something about it.

I want to commend you for portraying a young black male in a positive role. You give young people hope that they do not have to turn to drugs and crime to make a name for themselves. Black-on-black crime is reaching an all time high and a lot of it is the black youth hurting each other. I know this because it happens every day in my hometown.
—Sukrete

I feel you are a positive influence to young black youths. You show them that there are things out there other than partying and having a good time.
—Delise, 16

I thank you especially because plenty of young black men can look at you and see the importance of family love and studying. On the show you are a typical American family, and not stereotyped as a poor, unsuccessful black family.
—Carla

I feel that because of you the next generation can know that our young black youth have more to look forward to than unemployment, gangs, and drugs.
—Margie, 15

In a way I'm glad some kids get to thinking about race when they sit down to write to me. I know I said it bothers me, but that's only on one level. On another I recognize it's important to think about race and the relations among races, and too many kids avoid thinking about it. Adults too. And when people do think about it they all think their own thoughts. Everything is implied. No one talks about it, unless an incident like the one that happened at Howard Beach explodes in the papers, and then, as far as that community is concerned, it's too late.

We've got to get a dialogue going.

9

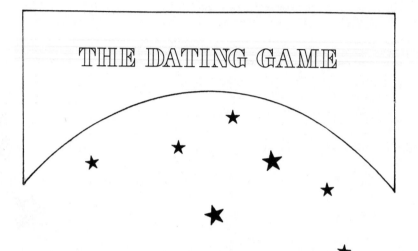

THE DATING GAME

NOTES ON TEENAGE DATING
AND SEXUALITY

How's your love life been treating you? Mine's okay, but could be better, if this boy will notice I'm alive.

—Stacey, 15

In school they don't teach you about sex. A lot of people talk about sex and if you've had it or not. Are you supposed to be ashamed if you're a virgin?

—Cal, 17

This one guy is ignoring me. I can't say his name but my friends know who I am talking

about. For one thing, he wants to have inter-course, but I'm not ready. He gets mad when you tell him no, and he leaves you, but then he comes back and tries the same thing.
—Deb, 15

Most likely over half the people that talk about sex don't know what they're talking about.
—Artie, 14

I'm in a tough position when it comes to talking about sex, mainly because of who I am and what I do. I've talked about this elsewhere in the book, but one of the things that comes with the territory when you're on a popular television series is that people see you as a role model. I've got to watch out for what I do and what I say, because, for whatever reason, other kids take me seriously, and that's something that I take seriously. Right or wrong, kids follow my lead, and I've got an obligation to "The Cosby Show" producers, to NBC, and also to everyone who watches the show to make sure that my lead is at least headed in the right direction.

But I'll be eighteen when this book is published, and that obligation also extends to everyone who's taken the time to write to me or to read this book, and so I've decided that the best way to treat such important subjects as dating and teenage sexuality is to be honest and open (at least a little bit). If the rest of this book is PG, then this chapter will just have to be rated PG-13.

First, let me tell you some of the things I don't do when it comes to girls. I'm not into hurting other people's feelings. I don't work that way and I never will work that way. A lot of girls equate sex with love, and a lot of times a guy tells a girl he loves her, and whatever else she wants to hear, and then he has sex with her, and then he leaves her. Or sometimes it happens the other way around. That's wrong. I hear about guys who do that sort of thing all the time, and when I hear about it I scratch them off my list of people I can respect. I hear about girls' treating guys the same way, and I feel the same way about them.

I don't like to move too quickly. I like it when things have some time to happen. Sometimes I'm with a girl who comes on too fast, or too strong, and I try to slow her down a couple of beats until we're at the same speed. Some of the best things in this world take time. I don't kiss a girl too soon because I don't want her to think that's all I'm about, or that it's all that I think she's about. Plus I think it's kind of exciting if you have things to look forward to, if you don't rush. You see, I was raised around women. A lot of my mother's friends were women, and they all had daughters. Also, I had a whole bunch of female cousins, and just a few male cousins. There were all these women around my house ever since I can remember, so all the time I'd be hearing about relationships from the girl's point of view and I picked up a few things on what girls like and don't like about guys.

I don't have a serious girlfriend. At other times in my life, I've been involved in exclusive relationships—you know how at fourteen and fifteen years old they can seem to be the most important thing in the world!—but that's not something I'm looking for now. I'm doing too many other things to be tied down in a serious way; it wouldn't be fair to me, and it wouldn't be fair to the girl. I just can't see taking myself out of circulation right now.

Also, I don't tell tales. I'm always hearing this locker room talk about so-and-so's sleeping with so-and-so, about who's good and who's not good, who's easy and who's not so easy. Sex is not something to be bragged about and dragged around in public; it's something that happens between two people and not between a girl and a guy and all of his friends. Or all of her friends. It shouldn't be a game where people compare notes.

I remember when I was twelve years old, living out in Los Angeles, and me and the guys would be hanging around the park, and I'd be swearing, "I'm not a virgin. I'm not a virgin." I mean, twelve years old, can you believe it! We were all doing that, and we were all lying. For whatever reason, from a very early age it was driven into us that sex was all about attitude, all about being cool. It's the same today, except I think now it starts at an even younger age. When you grow up you don't do that anymore. Oh, I know some guys older than I am who still act like twelve-year-old kids, but that's just because getting older doesn't necessarily mean you're also growing up.

The most important thing I don't do is take any chances. Take that to mean whatever you want, but no other generation yet has had to grow up in the terrifying shadow of AIDS, and no other generation has so selfishly contributed to the number of unwanted teenage pregnancies. You've got to be careful; nothing is worth being careless.

As for the things I do, well, as I said, I don't kiss and tell.

Also, I respect the person I'm with. That's not just a line; it's the truth, and I hope I get the same kind of respect in return.

I think it's very important to have a friend, a very special, very close friend of the opposite sex. I'm lucky enough to have that. I'm not talking about a physical relationship, but a trusting, honest friendship with someone you can open up to, someone you can be yourself with. A lot of my good friends are girls, and I have one terrific friend who helps me out whenever I'm on unfamiliar ground. She knows who she is. I'll call her up and she'll help me put things in perspective, or sometimes she'll call me up and I'll do the same for her. We can talk about anything. It helps to have someone to talk you through the rough spots, to let you know how it is you're supposed to behave, what's expected of you. And then there are the basics, the things that guys can never really know about girls, and girls can never really know about guys. A lot of times, if you're on a date or if you're alone with someone special, you're too embarrassed to talk. There's too much else going on. It's funny how two people can be physically intimate with each other and still be too shy to be emotionally intimate. Me and my friend, though, we can talk about things. She can explain to me what menstruation does to the rest of her body, or what it's like to wear a tampon, or she'll want to know what it feels like to have an erection, or why sex can feel different when you wear a condom.

If you have sex it should be right for you, not because everyone else is doing it.
—Jasmine, 19

I think kids today are more sexually active and I don't know how to feel about it. I mean I kind of want to have sex and I kind of don't want to have sex.
—Keith, 17

I'll keep this a secret, but do you think about sex? I don't, but do you?
—Bill, 14

Every time I meet a guy my friendship isn't important at all. That's the way it seems. If I invite them over for a visit they automatically think I want to be involved (sexually). I haven't met a guy yet who wants to be with me just for me. It's true. Do you know that it has gotten so bad I'm afraid to go out now because I think, "So, when he takes me home I wonder what I'm gonna have to do to show him I appreciated it."
—Esme, 18

Sex means a lot of different things to a lot of different people, but when you're in high school it can sometimes mean the wrong things. A lot of kids become sexually active just to prove that they're mature. They let their bodies get ahead of the rest of them and they run around saying, "Hey, I'm almost an adult; I can do whatever I want." They get a little out of control. Other kids go a little bit faster than they should as a way to get back at their parents, as a kind of rebellion. They think they're hurting their parents, or punishing them, by being sexually active before they're ready. Some kids are just curious and want to see what all the noise is about. And then there are some who are ready, who've got their heads on straight enough to handle it, and who are involved in a relationship with someone who's the same way. I've known all kinds and I get letters from all kinds.

> *When it comes to having sex with girls, well, if it is something that happens, then she was ready for it, but if there is even the slightest pause or hesitation then it is out of the question. I'm not like that.*
> —*Clark, 16*

> *I am almost eighteen and have never had a real date. It's a real problem. Everyone I ask is dating someone else. I only ask out the girls that are pretty and that have nice personalities, but they are pretty much spoken for by other guys.*
> —*Stephen, 17*

> *I'm very old-fashioned when it comes to love and dating. But I'm willing to change. If a girl asked you out on a date, would you think of her as a desperate person?*
> —*Deborah, 17*

> *I saw you on a show, just a week ago, and your mom was there too. Someone asked you have*

you lost your virginity yet, but you didn't an-
swer on the show. I did want to know. I think
you should have sex if it's out of love.
                                        —Stillman

It was pretty weird, but one of my most serious talks about sex with my mother took place on national television. I'm not kidding. I was a guest on "The Late Show," on Fox Television, and Arsenio Hall was the host, and he started asking me all kinds of personal questions. He brought my mom out from backstage and onto the couch with us, and he was going on and on about my sex life; he even came straight out and asked me if I was still a virgin! Man, for a minute there I didn't know who was more embarrassed, me or my mother, but then when I tried to dodge the question my mother came right back at me wanting to know the answer. Arsenio might have been willing to let me off the hook, but my mom sure wasn't. The audience was really into it, and Arsenio was making this big joke out of it, and I have to admit it was kind of funny, but underneath it all I was squirming and waiting for the show to be over. I was thinking, Great, I'm never going to hear the end of this.

It's funny, but after we did that show I could tell my mom wanted to finish our conversation. Eventually we did, but for a while we just kind of let the subject hang there between us. All that time I had a feeling she figured I knew what I was doing, or maybe she was just afraid that I knew what I was doing and she didn't want to know about it. Maybe the whole subject of sex, when it involves me, makes her uncomfortable. I know talking to her about it makes me uncomfortable. I was uncomfortable with it on national television (I noticed that my face looked pretty embarrassed when I played the videotape I had made of that show later!), and I'm uncomfortable with it anytime it comes up at home. But the important thing is it does come up at home. My mom and I talk about sex enough that each of us knows what the other is thinking, and we may be made uncomfortable by our talks, but that doesn't get in the way of our having them.

Things are a little different with my dad, but not much different. My father asked me once if I was a virgin, and I answered him, and that was it. End of conversation. It was as if he had never even asked the question. I think he heard what he didn't want to hear and then he put it out of his mind. I think my mom is the same way. She's great about being open with me about sex, but there are things about my sex life she probably doesn't want to hear, and so the only way to avoid hearing them is to avoid that topic of conversation. It would be cool to talk with my pop about girls and sex and everything, and probably someday we will, but I don't think my mom is in any rush to beat him to it.

In a way, though, my folks have talked to me very seriously about sex. It's kind of an unspoken conversation. They've taught me by example, by the way they've lived their own lives. They trust me, and they know that I'm smart enough about serious things to take care of myself. I know, pretty much, what they'd say to me if they sat me down, and they've got a good idea of what I'd say back. If they didn't feel that way I'm sure they'd suffer through all of our discomfort and give me a lecture every other night.

Dealing with parents when it comes to sex is hard, because you don't want to disappoint them, but then again you still want to experiment. You don't want to wake up one day and find that you're twenty-three years old and you still don't know what life's about. It's okay if you're still a virgin at twenty-three—that's not what I mean—it's just that at a certain age you should know what's what when it comes to sex.

I don't know how I'll be as a father, how I'm going to act. I may be more strict than my folks. I don't know, but it's possible. I can certainly understand their perspective. It must be hard trying to find a balance as a parent. You always want the best for your children. You don't want them to mess up. Right now my thinking is, it's okay if we make a few mistakes, but let us make the mistakes so we can learn from them. That might change when I'm on the other side of this problem, the parent's side, but for now that's how I feel.

Parents have a kind of line that they don't want their kids to cross, and that line seems to get blurred and redrawn as we get older. First, they tell you you're not ready to have a steady girlfriend or boyfriend. That lasts for about a year or so. They'll say they don't want you talking on the phone so much together, and they'll probably say it's because of the phone bill, but really it's because they don't know how else to handle the situation.

Then they don't want you kissing a girl or holding hands. Next, they don't like it when we bump up against each other in a slow dance, and after that they get nervous about the thought of any kind of passionate kissing or petting. Finally, they draw the line at intercourse, and even that line is erased after a while. I know that as I've progressed from one stage to the next, I've always heard a little voice—my mom's voice—in the back of my head, giving approval or disapproval. My friends tell me it's the same way for them. (I guess my mom's voice gets around.)

We did an episode of "The Cosby Show" that got pretty close to the way things really are between parents and kids when it comes to sex. A friend of Denise's was pregnant, and Theo's parents sat the kids down for a serious talk. The message was, you can always come to us, no matter what it is. But then the kids gave them all kinds of examples of situations—at one point Denise said she lied about spending a Saturday night at her girlfriend's house, and really spent the night with her boyfriend—and the parents got all upset. They really got hot about it, and then Denise said something like "You see, that's just an example, but if I came and really told you that, how could we even discuss it? You'd be so upset you'd ground me forever."

She's right. They would.

It's a double standard. Parents want you to tell them everything (not just about sex, but about other things too), but if you're like most kids you tell your parents only what you want them to hear. I know if I told my parents certain things they would flip out.

The way "The Cosby Show" producers answered this problem on the show was that the parents said something to the kids like "We don't get mad at you; we get mad at the situation." Or "We still love you; we just don't care for the situation." Maybe when I'm a parent I'll understand the difference, but for now it's all the same to me.

I can't understand why parents treat you the way they do. Like, my parents want me to be responsible, but I can't talk on the phone to boys. Heaven forbid if they ever catch me with someone.

—*Rhanda, 14*

When you're around old people if you say sex they gasp. They don't even face facts. Sex is becoming more and more common.

—*Hal, 13*

Malcolm, I got a lot of things on my mind about boys. A lot of people tell me once I get into high school boys will always try to talk to me. This boy across the street really likes me a lot, I mean a whole lot, but my father doesn't want me to have a relationship with him.

—*Rina*

But it's important for us to remember that our parents don't always have all the answers. Sometimes I even hear from one of them:

I am very proud of my daughter, except I need your help. She's fourteen and she's at that age where she thinks she needs to have sex to keep up with the crowd. I talk to her but it doesn't sink in. I think she would understand you more, coming from someone who is as big a star as you are and who is close to her age. You can call collect if you want, to let her know how important it is to stay a virgin until that special time comes (marriage). Could you do this for me?

—Genevieve

The thing that gets me about this last letter is that the woman went on to tell how she and her boyfriend were planning to get married after living together for four years. Now, I may be only eighteen, but it seems to me if this mom is so concerned about teaching her daughter the importance of virtue until that special time (marriage), she could stop a minute to look at the messages her own behavior might be sending. After all, monkey see, monkey do, right?

I think some parents, like the mom in this letter, are missing the point when it comes to teaching kids about sex. They set it up so sex becomes this big evil thing, and when you go about it that way there's a good chance the kid will go out and do exactly what you say not to do. It's like, if you're going to tell me what I can't do, then I'm going to go out and do it, simple as that.

Other parents come at the subject straight on. Some of my friends have parents who treat them as adults. They tell their kids if they're mature enough to have sex, they should have sex maturely. I know girls whose moms take them to be fitted for a diaphragm or get them a prescription for birth control pills, and I know guys whose dads buy them condoms. That's great. (I even know some moms who buy their daughters condoms.) My folks and I are not that way, and that's great too. An aunt of mine once gave me a box of condoms for Christmas, and my mom kind of kidded me about it, but I'm pretty sure there was a part of her that didn't make the leap to thinking I might actually have the chance to use them. I'm pretty sure if I told her I ran out of them and needed a new box she wouldn't know how to deal with it. She likes the idea that I'm aware enough to use a condom, but I think that's all she likes about it, the idea.

I think you've got to try on a bunch of different ways of dealing with each other before you hit on the way that's right for your family.

If you don't do it, everyone says you're a fag. Plus they have clubs around and if you don't have sex you can't be in this club because you're scared of girls. If you don't have sex with a girl and she wants you to, she will go back telling everybody and everyone in sight and they will talk about you, laugh at you, call you names you never have heard before.
—Rickey, 15

This letter is not about me needing a relationship with someone, because I don't believe in having a serious relationship with anyone at my age. I'm too young. But, I do believe in having friends, except sometimes people say you need to have one to have the other. Know what I mean?
—Camille, 16

Sometimes I get upset because I haven't had a boyfriend in a very long time. It's not lonely, it's just that everyone picks on me.
—Marietta

There is a tremendous amount of pressure on kids to date and to be sexually active. There's just no way to overstate that. I see it in the letters I get, and I see it in school, and I see it with my friends outside school. It's like the line I was talking about earlier, the one that parents draw. Kids draw their own lines too. At different ages, having a girlfriend or a boyfriend means different things; experimenting or being sexually active with a person of the opposite sex doesn't always mean having intercourse. When you're ten or twelve, it can mean kissing or holding hands or talking gushy on the phone; when you're thirteen or fourteen, it can mean making out and petting with your steady, or it can mean going out to a dance or a party together. By the time you're fifteen or sixteen, you've about run out of lines to cross. By that age, it's kind of expected that when you're out with a girl more than a few times, something will happen, sexually speaking, and if nothing happens then something's wrong. There is this tremendous added tension when you're out on a date, enough so that you start to wonder what the other one is thinking: Should I make a move? Is she expecting me to make a move? Why doesn't she make a move? What should be a private moment between two people becomes something much bigger, as if there's a crowd of people watching.

And because of all the pressure surrounding sex, there is also a lot of promiscuity. It's easier for kids to succumb to pressure than it is to fly in the face of it, and so you wind up with this whole mess of kids experimenting sexually when they don't really want to be experimenting sexually, when they're not ready. They're doing it because they think it's expected of them.

My best friend is a guy and he has dated this girl for eight months. I know for a fact they have sex. I am a senior and I haven't had a date for a year. I'm very good-looking (sorry, I'm not very humble), but I'm not promiscuous. I have not felt so pressured to have sex as I have this year, senior year. It seems, to get a date I need to promise something to the guy.
—Kaitlin, 17

Every time someone I'm interested in comes along, he has only one thing on his mind: sex and kissing. I, for one, would like to talk sometimes, or enjoy the surroundings other than him. What happened to conversation?
—Darlene, 17

Now, I'm not for teen sex one hundred percent. I don't believe in sex on a simple date, or for the fun of it, but how can someone tell us to abstain completely until we're married when everything (and everyone) else is saying it's okay?
—Andrea, 18

With me, there's a whole other ingredient I have to add to the mix. I've got to be honest with myself and figure out whether the girl I'm with is interested in me because of who I am or because of what I do. Face it, a lot of times girls are attracted to me because of "The Cosby Show." They get this idea in their heads that maybe I'm rich and famous, and they think some of it's going to rub off on them. Now, I'm not saying this is a good thing or a bad thing for me to have to deal with; it's just something I have to pay attention to. Girls talk just as much with their friends about their sexual exploits as guys do, and it doesn't sit right with me that some of the girls I date go back and tell their friends about me.

★ 117 ★

Sex leaves you vulnerable, particularly when you're young and you don't really know what you're doing and you lack a certain self-confidence, and it's lousy to think if you make a fool of yourself the news will spread faster than poison ivy. Everyone has to deal with this, in one way or another, but in my case it sometimes seems I play it extra careful so I always say and do the right thing.

But that's my problem. Other kids have other problems, and their problems are as big to them as mine are to me. A lot of times I look up from a pile of mail and feel as if I'm in the middle of a school soap opera.

A year ago I fell in love with my best friend (a totally self-destructive move), and then tried to back off in an effort to save our friendship. It worked, at least I think so, but I wasn't sure if he still hung on waiting for another chance with me or simply to be my friend.
—Stephanie, 16

I have a girlfriend I love. Mindy is her name. Mindy does not love me. I think she knows who I am, but I'm pretty sure she doesn't love me.
—Alex, 11

I am 15 years old and my boyfriend is 17. We have been going together for about a year, and for the first nine months he constantly pressured me to have sex with him. About a month ago, I gave in. It was my first time. I am not sure whether it was because of the pressure, or because I wanted to. You are the only other person that knows this. We are still together and better than ever, and I think that I am only lucky. That's the only reason. I have many friends whose relationships were broken up because of sex.

—Cindy, 15

I don't have a boyfriend but I like two guys. They both like me. See, one of 'em has a girlfriend, so I'm next. The other one, I'm too shy to talk to him, but he said he's gonna write me a note! Sweet, huh? I think so!
                                            —Zoreen, 15

This guy Andy, who happens to be the biggest nerd in school, asked me out for the third time this year. Why do I always get the nerds?
                                            —Alicia, 17

I have been involved with this guy for a year and a couple of weeks and it seems like everyone wants to see us apart. The girls in school talk about me and they try to upset me.
                                            —Felice, 17

I want to address two subjects that were not adequately addressed in my mail. The first is masturbation. Stay with me here, because this is tough to talk about, but it is important to talk about it. There is nothing wrong with masturbation. It's perfectly right and normal and healthy. It's a part of growing up sexually. I mean, you have to learn about yourself as a sexual being before you can have sex with someone else, right? And besides, sex doesn't come any safer than this.

I was also planning to devote a whole section of this chapter to a discussion of AIDS and teenagers, but when I looked back over the letters I've saved I was surprised to see I haven't heard from more kids about it, or about the fear of casual sex that's running rampant now in the single and sexually active adult community.

But then when I stopped to think about it some more, it started to make sense. Look, right or wrong, when I'm sitting around with my friends, the subject of AIDS hardly comes up at all. It's not that all these media campaigns for

★ 119 ★

public awareness haven't hit home—I think they have—it's just that it's not talked about. I don't know why that is, but that's the way it is. Maybe it's because as kids we feel sort of invincible—you know, immortal—that nothing can touch us. Maybe it's because we feel we're in our own special world and the problems plaguing the rest of the world, the real world, can never invade our space and affect us. Maybe it's because we don't like the fact that adults have made this world a screwed-up place to live, and so maybe we choose to ignore the lousy deal we've been handed, figuring maybe if we ignore it, it will go away.

Maybe it's because we're naïve. (Probably it's because we're naïve.)

Whatever the reason, judging from my mail and from my friends, AIDS is not as much on the minds of today's teenagers as you might expect, certainly not as much as it should be. I've read newspaper and magazine articles about AIDS that say the same thing. "Safe sex" has become a slogan, and it's registered on some level, but on another level it's just a slogan. Sure, kids are using condoms now, more than ever before, but I get the feeling the increase has more to do with birth control—or at least as much to do with birth control—than it does with a fear of any sexually transmitted disease.

Certainly kids aren't cutting back any with their sexual behavior, not from where I sit. The rest of the world may be cutting back, but high school kids are still going at it as if they invented it. You wouldn't believe the amount of bed hopping that goes on. A lot of times I could be sitting in a room with a bunch of guys and a bunch of girls and it's possible that half of one group has, at one time or another, slept with half of the other. That's the way it seems sometimes. Or, I get an earful of some locker-room conquest talk, and a lot of times the guys are comparing notes about the same girl, or the girls about the same guy.

So here's my bulletin from the front: teenagers are still having sex, lots of it. That's the way it is, and the national panic surrounding AIDS has yet to make a serious dent in most high schools. It's made a subconscious dent, I think, but it's not a subject that's in the air or on our minds as much as it should be. Oh, there are AIDS-education and AIDS-awareness classes being taught everywhere you turn, but despite all that attention kids don't seem to think about AIDS as something that can happen to them.

Man, do we still have a few things to learn!

The few letters I do get about AIDS, and the fear of AIDS, don't even scratch the surface of the problem.

Sometimes I wonder if I have gotten AIDS by a way scientists haven't discovered.
—Joshua, 15

I have so many girls that is liking me. You know I have to have sex with all of them, but when I do I feel I might get something from one of them.
—Eddie, 17

The thing about AIDS is it can just find you without your knowing about it. That's all. There's not a lot you can do.
—Cynthia, 11

AIDS is certainly fixed somewhere in the back of our minds—sometimes it seems every other news item is another horrifying AIDS-related statistic—but for most kids it never comes out front and center. If you asked any kid, on any school bus, he'd tell you he was very worried about AIDS, sure, who isn't? But the thing is, that worry doesn't translate into anything. It hasn't changed his behavior any. He thinks AIDS is something for his parents to worry about, or his teachers, or his bachelor uncle. (By the way, it's not just AIDS; we also need to worry about herpes, gonorrhea, syphilis, venereal warts, chlamydia, and other sexually transmitted diseases.)

Mostly, I guess, we've got other things to worry about, and I'm not sure if our other worries are more important or not. I mean, clearly they're not, but it's nice in a way that we can go on with the rest of our lives despite AIDS. In a way I like it that the rest of the world is frantic with concern about AIDS, and somehow we're able to hold onto enough of what's special about growing up so that AIDS doesn't interfere with it. I don't know about you, but I'd feel cheated if we weren't given the same chances as our parents before us, though, I know, they had a lot of other, different restrictions growing up. I'm not saying this to diminish the impact of AIDS on our sexual behavior, or to suggest that kids shouldn't pay a whole lot more attention to what is clearly a very serious, very deadly problem. But it is a small comfort, a silver lining, that things haven't gotten to the point where we're too scared to experiment and explore and grow up sexually, as long as we are selective about those we choose to give our love to. Yes, the young adult population is at tremendous risk of contracting AIDS, as much as the rest of the population, but because of AIDS we are also at tremendous risk of losing something very unique and wonderful about our adolescence. That hasn't happened yet.

And yet even in the darkening shadow of AIDS, the problems between the sexes are in many ways the same for today's teenagers as they were for kids in our parents' generation, and in the generations before that. We can still experiment and explore and grow up sexually, as long as we use condoms and choose our partners carefully. I know that even these precautions won't protect us one hundred percent, but right now they're the best we can do.

I want to know if you can give me pointers on how to get the girl I really love.
—Brett, 13

★ 122 ★

Since high school, I've dated several girls seriously. I like going out with other couples, you know, doubling. But recently a problem has developed. The couples we are with will sometimes suddenly start making out. When I see this, I can't even look at my date, even if I've dated her for several months. What am I expected to do?
—*Jess*

I know you receive millions of letters every day, but I believe this letter is slightly different. I'm very shy and it took a lot of nerve for me to write you this letter. In March, our school is having the annual Junior/Senior Prom and I need a date. I know this seems unusual, but I don't know anyone else I can ask. Could you let me know right away, because otherwise I'll have to go with my cousin.
—*Nellie, 17*

The only advice I can really give is, just be yourself. Be careful and be yourself. Do what feels right. Pay attention to AIDS and other sexually transmitted diseases and pay attention to birth control and pay attention to your parents. Don't pay any attention to what your friends say about what you should be doing, or how you should be doing it. And parents, pay attention to your kids. At least give us some room to make decisions for ourselves. You can help us draw the lines for our sexual behavior, but it's up to us if and when we're going to cross those lines. I know it sounds obvious and corny, but I'm not Dr. Ruth and it's the best I can do. And *please,* be careful.

10

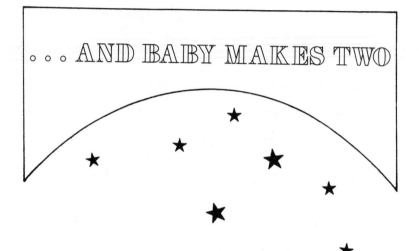

... AND BABY MAKES TWO

NOTES ON TEENAGE PREGNANCY

Here's what a lady said when she came to talk to our school. She said girls use their bodies to get love and boys use their bodies to get power. That's the way I see it too.

—Kim, 15

This is something that might be interesting to you. My mother had me when she was 14. She didn't finish high school until I was in school. I've never seen my father, not even a picture.

—Lisa, 12

*Do you think teenage girls get themselves preg-
nant in order to keep the boy? How do you feel
about guys leaving the girls when the situation
is at hand?*
                                              —Maya, 14

*In the morning I take care of the baby and then
my mother takes over when I go to school, and
then when I come home I take over from her. At
night when the baby's sleeping I sleep too, or I
do my homework, but sometimes he's up all
night long fussing. I don't hardly see my
friends anymore. And my boyfriend, you can
forget about him.*
                                         —Constance, 15

Let me start out with some encouraging news. Teenage
pregnancies in the United States are finally on the de-
crease. We still have a long way to go, but we're moving
in the right direction; for the first time in a long time the
numbers are on the way down.

Okay, so that's a good sign. What it tells us is that the
sex education courses and free contraceptives programs
are making some kind of difference, that they're impacting
on their communities. That's a terrific positive and I'm
glad to hear it's taking, but despite the recent decline, the
United States still leads almost all developed nations in
teenage pregnancy, childbearing, and abortion rates. The
pregnancy rate among American teenagers is two times as
high as the British, French, and Canadian rates; it's three
times the Swedish rate, and seven times the Dutch rate.
(Planned Parenthood, which produces some helpful litera-
ture on this subject, is the source of all the statistics in this
chapter.)

The numbers are still too high. As far as I'm concerned, they're through the roof. One unwanted teenage

pregnancy would make the numbers still too high. The fact is, districtwide or even nationwide programs can have a positive affect on statistics, can even help turn around a trend, but each single, isolated incident can make all the numbers meaningless. A fifteen-year-old pregnant girl in the Bronx, with no support from her family or her boyfriend's family, doesn't care diddly about the decline in the teenage pregnancy rate. She's got her own situation to worry about.

You can play with the numbers and make them tell you anything you want. And so despite the recent decline, when you break them down, they are still alarming. In New Jersey, for instance, there were 10,018 births among girls age fifteen to nineteen in 1985, the last year for which statistics are available. That means that more than three percent of all girls in that age group had babies that year —three percent! That figure seems astonishingly high to me, and it doesn't even take into account all the pregnancies that were aborted or not carried to term.

Nationally, the numbers are even worse. Each year, 1.1 million girls, age fifteen to nineteen, become pregnant in this country. That translates into one girl out of every eleven, and to one out of every four girls in that age group who are sexually active. One in five new mothers each year is a teenager. And our young mothers are keeping their babies after they have them: at last count, 1.3 million babies were being raised by 1.1 million teenage mothers.

I don't care what the numbers say; we still have a long way to go.

I live in Chicago, Illinois, and there are three schools to my knowledge that are distributing contraceptives to their students for free. I think that is a smart move on their part, because over fifty percent of their female students were pregnant, or something like that.

—Janine, 17

Girls who get pregnant usually don't mind.
Usually they like having sex and it's the boys
who can't handle it, or didn't really know what
they were doing, or didn't use the right thing.
                                        —Katey, 15

One or two of my friends have had intercourse
without any form of birth control, in spite of
the ease of obtaining it, and in spite of the AIDS
and venereal disease warnings. One of them
became pregnant and missed a year of school to
have the child. Is that one small chance worth
it?
                                        —Suzette, 14

I get a lot of letters from kids repeating some of the
basic myths about birth control. You'd think that after
years of sex education and public service announcements
on television and explicit frankness in movies and music,
some truths would sink in, but some kids are surprisingly
thick-skulled about these things.

Let me clear up a few things for you. You can't get
pregnant from sitting on a toilet seat, but you *can* get
pregnant if you have intercourse during your period. You
can also get pregnant during other times of vaginal bleed-
ing. There are no "safe" times to have sex without fear of
pregnancy. No matter what you may have heard, or what
your friends tell you, it's possible to get pregnant when you
are ovulating, and it's impossible to tell exactly when you
are ovulating; you may think you know, but even your
doctor can never be one hundred percent sure. Also, it is
entirely possible to get pregnant the very first time you
have intercourse. (I can't tell you how many times I've
heard this last one.) You can get pregnant if you have sex
standing up, or if you jump up and down after sex, or if
you have sex in a moving vehicle. Let's face it, with sex
comes the risk of pregnancy.

Girls, you can get pregnant before you even have your first period, and you can get pregnant even if you don't have an orgasm during intercourse. And here's another one: don't buy that line you hear from guys about how you'll do them horrible physical harm if they don't ejaculate when they're sexually aroused. It's just a line.

Now, I don't mean to offend anyone with talk of birth control, but I think it is necessary here. Stop reading this chapter if it bothers you. Here goes: There is no form of birth control, other than abstinence, that is one hundred percent effective. Condoms come close, a diaphragm even closer, and the pill closest of all. There are also some jellies and creams and sponges you can use alone, or to increase the effectiveness of other methods. Some educators counsel kids to use more than one method of birth control to reduce the risk. That's not a bad idea, although often you'll find that condoms and jellies and creams are the only affordable and accessible methods available to most kids. (I've known some guys who've worn two condoms at a time, even three, which might be safer than one but certainly a lot less comfortable.) Girls, some forms of birth control need to be prescribed or fitted by a doctor. If you're going to be sexually active, you should see a gynecologist regularly.

Douching with Coke or Sprite or Dr Pepper, or any other carbonated beverage, is not an effective form of birth control. Wine coolers don't work either. Neither does a stretch of Saran Wrap wrapped around the penis; it may be resourceful, but it's certainly not effective.

Birth control is not the girl's responsibility, nor is it the guy's responsibility. It is a joint responsibility: shared. Both of you should worry about it and both of you should do something about it. Neither of you should take for granted that the other will handle it.

Guys, here's one for you: It is possible to get a girl pregnant even if you don't ejaculate inside her. Withdrawal is just about the least effective of all methods of birth control. Most times you can secrete a small amount of semen without even knowing it; you might think you're pulling out in time, but you're not. Plus, we all know how easy it is to give in to temptation. Nature is telling your body not to pull out and even if your head is telling you what you have to do, nature will almost always win. Even if nature doesn't win there's still a good chance you'll have lost.

Learn the facts because if you don't you'll have to live with more than just a baby.

Why are people so high on rumors? Last year, one of my best friends had sex with a very popular kid in our school and then the guy decided to brag to his friends. By the end of the week, people she didn't even know were saying she was pregnant. Of course, for the guy nothing was wrong, it was even cool, but for my friend, people called her a slut and other names. Guys would ask her why she wouldn't share with them.

—Larissa, 15

My sister has a baby which her boyfriend is not happy to raise. She's seventeen. I want them to move out of our house. I'm tired of them being there.

—Bobby, 12

I have a friend that's twenty now and she has three kids. She had her first one when she was fourteen. I can understand making a mistake once, but three times? I couldn't see myself becoming pregnant now, no way. I can't take care of myself so how can I take care of a baby?

—Rose, 14

For what it's worth the grapevine is in fuller bloom among teenagers than it is among adults. Kids like to talk, and the things they like to talk about most of all are the mistakes made by other kids. I'm amazed at the way certain intimate details are thrown all the way out in the open for peer inspection. Kids today trade gossip the way they used to trade baseball cards, and teenage pregnancy is at the top of the list of hot topics. If a girl is pregnant, sometimes it seems that the whole school knows about it. If she has an abortion, that news also makes the rounds. And, if she decides to have the baby, well, it's stop the presses.

Another observation: I realize it's important to have a friend to talk to, especially in times of crisis, but you have to be extremely careful about choosing the people you talk to. Find one special, trusted friend and leave it at that. You don't want news of your condition getting around any faster than it has to. It will get around, believe me, but you don't want to accelerate the process. And kids can be cruel. The mood of the classroom, from what I'm getting, is that pregnancy changes the way a teenage girl is treated by her schoolmates throughout the rest of her high school career. Even if the pregnancy is aborted and the girl returns to her normal routine, the news of her situation, and her solution to her situation, will always follow her around like a cloud. The same is sometimes true for the guy involved, but it is true to a much smaller degree.

Also, according to these letters, parents are the last to know about a lot of things. If you're pregnant, or if you've gotten your girlfriend pregnant, you've got to quickly get past the stage where you tell your parents, or where you can tell an adult in a position to help. You can take a day or two, or even a week, to take a deep breath and figure out what everything means, but don't take too long. The longer you wait, the deeper the hole you dig for yourself. No matter what your decision, there are steps you have to take to make sure that decision is carried out properly and maturely. If you're going to keep the baby, you have to be seen regularly by a doctor, both for your health and for your baby's: complications from pregnancy and birth lead to death among girls under sixteen at a rate 2.5 times greater than among women age twenty to twenty-four; also, girls under fifteen expose their unborn children to the risks of a low birth weight and perinatal death. If you're going to have an abortion, you have to act sooner rather than later; the procedure becomes more complicated as the pregnancy progresses. If you're going to give up the baby for adoption, you should talk to the appropriate agencies in your community to see about benefits and procedures; you might be able to find a program that will subsidize your costs and ensure you receive proper care.

Above all, find a way to tell your parents. They might be mad—for all I know that could be a grand understatement—but you've got to give them the benefit of the doubt on this one. You might be surprised that they'll be able to see past their anger and offer help. Even if that help only comes in the form of financial support, not emotional support, that's help enough.

Parents, get the message across to your kids that they can come to you with any problem, even one that's as big as this. That's the only way you'll hear from your kids when they're in this kind of trouble.

I'm concerned about teen pregnancy. Babies having babies, is what they call it. I see what goes on. A baby can't develop and sustain good health on Twinkies, soda, and potato chips. I think teenagers should think of themselves as a mother when they become sexually active.
—Lucinda, 17

I'm so worried because a lot of my girlfriends are having babies and a lot of my boyfriends

*have sexually transmitted diseases. Sometimes
I feel as if it's my turn next.*
—*Carol, 15*

*If teenagers decide to become sexually active,
they should have the common sense to protect
themselves. Lots of my friends have abortions
because they don't protect themselves.*
—*Diannah, 14*

*I have seventy dollars saved which I can use if
my girlfriend gets into trouble, but I don't
think it will be enough.*
—*Davis, 16*

One of the things that's most troubling to me in the
letters I receive is the widespread notion of abortion as a
kind of birth control. I see it among some of the kids I
know as well. There is a notion out there that if all else
fails, you can always have an abortion. It's that notion
which gets kids to thinking they can take some chances,
that if they get caught up in the heat of a moment they can
let the moment play itself out because if anything happens
they'll have time to worry about it later.

I'm not going to get into a moral or religious discussion of abortion. This is not the place for it, and I'm not in
any position to make a stand one way or the other. But
right or wrong, abortion is clearly not simply an extreme
form of birth control, no matter how you look at it. Yes,
it can solve the problem of an unwanted pregnancy, but it
can also mess up your body. I don't mean to scare anybody
who has had or who will have an abortion, but it is a
surgical procedure and no surgical procedure is without at
least the possibility of complications. That's something
that's not stressed enough. People walk around thinking,
"Well, the worst thing that can happen is I'll get an abor-

tion," but that's not the worst thing that can happen. The worst is that you'll get an abortion that's not done properly and will cause some serious internal damage. Or, more likely, you might not be able to have another kid when you're older, when you're ready for it, when you want it.

No matter how much you pay for it or where you go to get it, an abortion is not easy on your body, and repeated abortions may do some damage to your reproductive system. They may also increase the possibility of premature births and miscarriages in later pregnancies. An abortion is not as simple or harmless a procedure as people think it is, particularly if you can't afford to go to a good clinic or doctor. Now, don't get me wrong; there are some wonderful free and inexpensive clinics in this country which are set up to handle abortions for girls who have no place else to turn. We need those places, but it's a fact of life that some are less wonderful than others. You have to be careful about where you go, and you have to be careful about how often you go. You can't keep undergoing a procedure like that and expect to keep coming out on the other side of it as good as new.

This idea of abortion as a kind of retroactive birth control pops up everywhere, in my mail and in the rest of my life. I know a girl—she's a friend of a friend—who had two or three abortions, and when she went in for one the last time the doctor told her that with her history she had the choice of not having this next abortion or jeopardizing her future ability to conceive and give birth. She chose to have the child. I feel bad for that girl, but she made the same mistake over and over and over again, and her story pokes all kinds of holes in the notion of abortion as birth control.

That notion has proved extremely tough to shake. According to Planned Parenthood, in New York City, where I live, roughly two-thirds of the fifteen thousand teenage girls who get pregnant each year undergo abortions.

That's ten thousand abortions! I have to think that number would be significantly lower if kids didn't always think of abortion as a viable means of birth control.

Somebody, please help me get this message across.

In some cases, abortion should be allowed, but in others such as teenage pregnancy, it should not. This is my opinion. If people would just stop and think for a second instead of letting the moment take, maybe a lot more problems can be solved.

—Daphne, 17

I am not condoning sex because I believe it shouldn't be done, but I also believe that if sex happens, then it's probably really important to a person. If it happens to you, then you should be responsible for it. Nobody's gonna take care of it for you.

—Rebecca, 15

You find more teenage girls pregnant than you do older women. The boys do nothing but persuade the girls to go to bed with them without using any protection. Then, he refuses to take full responsibility and she'll end up never seeing him again.

—Joanna

It's funny, the signals we send. I remember when I was living in Los Angeles, there was a girl in my junior high school who was pregnant. Everybody knew about it. Eventually, she was even visibly pregnant, very visibly pregnant, so, looking back, it seems she must have been past the point where she could safely have an abortion. I was only twelve years old, and yet I knew exactly what was going on. The whole school knew. I remember everyone kind of felt sorry for the girl, but nobody ridiculed her or shunned her in any way. Even at twelve, I was able to pick up that one of the reasons kids felt sorry for her was that they thought it could just as easily have happened to them. I see the same reaction now. Underneath the letters from the kids who write to me about their friends' troubles is the relief that they didn't happen to them. Underneath the gossip I pick up on among the kids I know is the same feeling, that they all feel lucky to have avoided the same fate, so far.

What gets me, though, is that kids don't do enough to avoid that same fate. At least they don't do as much as they can. It's true that teenagers are using contraception more than ever before, but that use can be incredibly inconsistent. A condom on Friday night can turn into Saran Wrap on Saturday night, and nothing at all by the next weekend. Plus, most kids don't use any form of birth control at all when they first become sexually active. Planned Parenthood reports that most teenagers wait through about six months of sexual activity before they seek counseling on birth control. I'm guessing there are a lot of chances taken in those first six months.

Let me finish up the story of that girl in junior high school. At some point, she stopped going to school. I never saw her again, and I never heard about what happened to her, and eventually everyone stopped talking about her, but somehow I think I came away with the idea that if you get pregnant in junior high school you'll be sent away. I think I saw what happened to her as a kind of punishment. To me that was the message.

We send our messages by example, and there's a big group of kids out there who get the wrong signals regarding teenage pregnancy from their parents, the very people whose attitudes you'd expect to be sound. Sometimes I even get letters from young parents who worry about the messages they send their own children; they're deeply concerned that their kids won't avoid making the same mistakes that they made.

> *Malcolm, how do I tell my little girl what to do and what not to do when she knows I had to leave high school to have her?*
> *—Jacqueline*

> *It's a different time from when I was in high school. I don't want my little girl to do the things I used to do.*
> *—Gwen, 31*

> *My mom looks good. She's only 27, and when we go out people say we look like sisters. She was pretty young when she had me and she says she loves me but she wishes she had me later.*
> *—Renata, 13*

When the new federal figures on teenage pregnancies were released in 1987, *The New York Times* ran an editorial which pointed out that among teenagers in Sweden, the Netherlands, France, Canada, England, and Wales, the fertility and abortion rates were far lower than in the United States, despite the fact that average ages at first sexual experience in all those countries are roughly the same. The paper referred to contraception as a "dirty secret" in many parts of the country.

I think that's changing a little bit, at least from where I sit. Kids today are better prepared than ever before for life in a changed world. Contraception is not a dirty secret anymore. There is a higher awareness regarding birth control than there was when our parents were growing up, than there was even five years ago. Kids are not afraid to talk about sex and sexually transmitted diseases with their family doctor. That's a side effect of the current AIDS scare. Every guy I know carries a condom in his wallet. A lot of girls carry them in their purses. Now, if we could just use them with more consistency, we should be okay. Because of the media attention focused on the AIDS crisis, using a condom has become almost a given in any sexual encounter among teens. It's expected. Great. Now, guys might be wearing them for selfish reasons, for self-preservation, but the point is that they are wearing them more often than ever before. Who cares why they're wearing raincoats, just as long as they're on when they should be? That's what counts, and maybe next time when they sit down to count up the number of teenage pregnancies the new statistics will reflect that. I hope so.

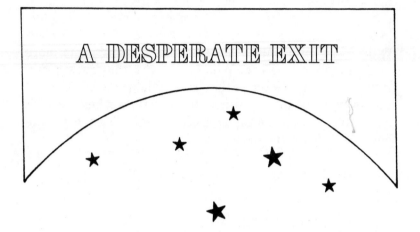

11

A DESPERATE EXIT

NOTES ON TEENAGE SUICIDE AND DEPRESSION

Sometimes I feel like getting into bed and never getting up. I get depressed a lot, but I really don't talk seriously to anyone. You talk to your friends, and then they turn on you, so I don't say anything.

—Beth, 16

It's hard being a teenager today. All we can do is hold on for dear life and hope our family and friends are there for us, no matter where we go or what we do.

—Kirk, 17

I've always thought about how I wish we can pick an age and stay that age for the rest of our life. I hate it that I have all this new stuff to worry about, but it makes me sick when I think about dying.

—Coleena, 16

Okay, now we're getting into the letters that give me some trouble. Real trouble. They'll probably give you some trouble too. Now, don't get me wrong. I don't mean that these notes give me trouble because they're not easy to read (they're not, by the way), but because I don't know how to respond, or if it's even appropriate that I respond. I mean, I'm no authority on depression; I'm just a kid who's going through the motions like everyone else.

Teenage suicide and depression are serious business, and I'll be the first to admit that maybe I'm in over my head here with these letters, but I do feel a certain responsibility to the kids who were in enough pain to write them. The kids who write to me see me as a friend, a willing ear, and when they pour out their problems I can't turn away from them. Most of the letters I get in this area, like many you'll see in this chapter, are from kids who seem to be thinking clearly, even if just a little bit clearly; who seem to be able to see beyond and through whatever desperate situation they're in. Sometimes, though, I hear from someone who is in a real bad situation, someone who definitely needs some immediate help. But how do you help perfect strangers from long distance? If there's a return address, I try to get in touch with them, to let them know there is at least one person they can talk to, to try to convince them to talk to somebody in their area who's in a better position to help them. But it's tough to reach out to someone when all you have to go by is a first name and a postmark. Once or twice I've gotten a note back, thanking me for being there for them, but it's more often the case that I can't offer any help at all, or that the help I do offer is never acknowledged or, more likely, never received.

I don't know what my responsibility is when I get a letter, say, from a seventeen-year-old cheerleader in Pennsylvania, who tells me she's pregnant by one of the football players—she doesn't know which one—and she can't talk to her friends because word is around she was easy with the football team and nobody takes her seriously; and she can't talk to her parents because they're strict and religious and wouldn't understand; and she can't talk to her brother or sister because she's afraid they'd tell her parents. What do I do when she tells me, "Malcolm, I can't show my face around here anymore?" I'm not trained to handle a situation like this, but I'm presented with situations like it all the time.

Now, don't go looking for any pregnant seventeen-year-old cheerleaders in Pennsylvania, because that's just a composite of some of the situations I've heard, but what can I offer a girl in that kind of mess? What can I say to a guy who feels his parents don't understand him? Or to a teenage girl who has to move to a new town because her mother just died and there's no one at home to take care of her? I can be a friend—a lot of times that is a good start, but really it's not nearly enough. In the case of our composite cheerleader, she needs to talk to a guidance counselor in her school, or a teacher, or some kind of helping adult in her community. She's got a problem that won't go away, one that, literally, will get bigger and bigger.

But a lot of what gets kids depressed and thinking about suicide can be brought down to size. Let's talk about some worst-case scenarios. You're pregnant, or you've gotten your girlfriend pregnant; you can't keep up in school; you're worried that you won't get into college, or that your parents can't afford to send you to college; you're always the odd man out at parties or, worse, you're never invited to any parties; your parents fight all the time or, worse, they don't even talk to each other; you've been sexually or emotionally abused; you've moved to a new town and you just don't fit in; your best friend was killed in a car accident and, worse, you were driving; you've totaled your parents' car.

I've had letters about all of these worst-case scenarios, and then some, and yet each and every problem has a viable solution. No exceptions. Sure, things may be tough for a while, for a long while even, but if you go about it right and smart they'll get better, slowly, at first, but believe me they'll get better. Remember, there are no easy answers, but there are answers.

> *Have you ever known a person who wished to die? Well, now you do. It's a very scary feeling when you have no direction. Life is a negative word, living is a negative concept. Dying is a very attractive thought, like the eye of the hurricane.*
> *—Andrew, 17*

> *I would never want to kill myself. I want to live forever.*
> *—Adrianne, 19*

> *I'm not afraid of death, but I am afraid of suicide. That may sound weird, but I had one friend who attempted suicide. She didn't succeed and I can't say whether I'm thankful or not. I feel responsible for her.*
> *—Charlene, 15*

I did a show once, an ABC After School Special, called "A Desperate Exit," and it must have hit some kind of chord, because after that show aired I got a whole wave of letters from depressed kids, from parents who've lost touch with their children (and, tragically, from some who've lost their children), from friends who've thanked me for opening their eyes to what their friends were going through. The show aired several years ago and I still get letters about it.

Now, I didn't do much more in "A Desperate Exit" than read somebody else's lines, but I did learn something from taking on that role. I played this character, Charlie, who is going with this girl whose parents don't want her to see him anymore. She's rich, he's not, her parents are college-educated, his are not, that kind of thing. Also, he is nervous about getting a scholarship to college, because without the scholarship his parents can't afford to send him, and he has all kinds of pressures on him from his mom, who thinks the straight A's he's pulling in aren't good enough. No one thing is enough to put Charlie over any kind of edge, but taken together they're beginning to exert a tremendous pressure, a burden. There's a lot going on, a lot for him to think about.

The clincher is one afternoon, when Charlie is having a secret romantic picnic with his girlfriend and he sees a girl he sort of knows from school teeter dangerously close to the edge of a cliff overlooking the ocean. Charlie's girlfriend right away worries that they've been seen, that someone will tell her parents they were together, but Charlie's worried about the girl from school. Something looks not right about her; she looks as if she's in trouble. He races over to her, he wants to help her, and she is so wasted she's almost passing out. She's really stoned. He doesn't know what she's on, or what she's up to, but he wants to put her in his girlfriend's car and take her somewhere for help. His girlfriend, meanwhile, doesn't want any part of this other girl; she cares more about not getting caught with Charlie than she does about helping a classmate obviously in trouble.

Charlie's pretty much torn, and the girl from school is pretty much out of it—she's all but passed out—and so he covers her with a blanket and figures he'll race back to her on his moped after his girlfriend drops him off at home. Let her get home safely and he'll come back and take care of it, he's thinking. But by the time he returns all that's left on the spot is the blanket, and he starts looking frantically for the girl from school. He finds her shoe at the edge of the cliff, and at that point the viewers, and Charlie, pretty much know what's happened. She jumped, or she fell—it's never made clear—but the point is, she's gone.

Charlie blames himself, and on top of everything else it all seems to be too much for him to handle. He can't talk to his girlfriend, because she's part of the problem; he can't talk to his parents, because they wouldn't understand; he can't talk to his teachers, because he knows they'll be disappointed in him and the decisions he made. He's got a best friend (played by Rob Stone from "Mr. Belvedere"), but he can't do much more than send out signals to him that's he's hit some kind of rough spot. He's got nowhere to turn, and so Charlie withdraws deeper and deeper into himself until eventually he hangs himself. That's his desperate exit.

The whole point of the show, though, is not the drama of Charlie's situation, but the way his friends and family deal with his death. The story is told in a kind of flashback, and it's all about how Charlie, who blamed himself for the girl's death, leaves behind friends and family who blame themselves for his. In retrospect they see signals that should have meant something to them.

There are two lessons here, at least the way I see it. The first is that no matter how big and deep your problem, there are ways to deal with it and there are people to help you deal with it. The problems, and the feelings of helplessness and hopelessness, are temporary. If you ask me, that's the easy lesson, the one taught in nearly every high school suicide prevention program in the country. The second lesson is much harder (and it affects a lot more people): even though it is your obligation as a friend to be on the watch for signs of depression, it is not your fault if you don't catch on. It's said that suicide is a selfish act, and behind every attempt you can find dozens of friends and teachers and family members who will wonder if there was anything they could have done to prevent it. So what we have here is a double-edged sword. Yes, it's your job to help out a buddy in a rough spot, but if you don't notice in time, you can't blame yourself.

That's the lesson learned by Charlie's best friend, who by the end of the show makes a kind of peace with Charlie's death. The last scene has him on the beach, flying Charlie's prized kite, and then at the very end he lets go of the string and the kite flies aimlessly in the air. To me it meant that he was letting go of the guilt he felt about Charlie, and that he was getting on with his own life.

> *I saw that show you did about suicide. I am glad it wasn't really you who committed suicide, but just a character you were playing. Things are going so good for you, you'd be stupid to try it. Me, though, things aren't so good.*
>
> —*Hector, 16*

> *Sometimes I might say, "If I don't make it into such-and-such high school I'll just die," but now after I've seen your show I'd take that back and hope never to say or do that ever. I feel sorry for all the people that believe there's no way out, but just to stop living altogether. My mom always says, "Life's too short." Well, now I'm going to do the best I can and try to get the most out of it.*
>
> —*Cindy, 13*

> *Today I saw that special and I cried at the end. It was the best ever. Okay, so after seeing it I now understand there's more to life than just good grades, or what group you're in, popular*

(LEFT) In our first New York apartment with Miriam Baum, my agent, 1984.

(BELOW) This picture of me in my room ran in People *magazine in 1984.*

(RIGHT) *Receiving an award at Youth in Film along with David Hollander, 1984.*
(BELOW) *I was grand marshal at a parade in Pittsburgh and got to ride in the back of a car, 1985.*

(LEFT) After the parade they took me and my mom to a Pittsburgh Pirates baseball game, 1985. (BELOW) Mom and Five Star (one of my favorite groups) paid me a surprise visit on "The Cosby Show" set, 1985.

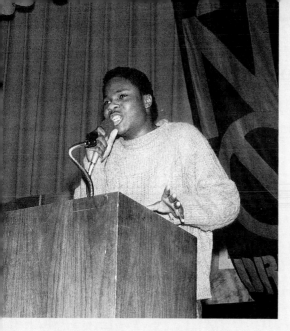

(LEFT) Talking to kids at Wells High School in Chicago, 1986.

(OPPOSITE, TOP) I met Jesse Jackson and his son while co-hosting Chicago's Bud Biliken Parade, 1987.

(OPPOSITE, BOTTOM) Having some fun with Marie Osmond and John Schneider during the Children's Miracle Network Telethon, 1987.

(BELOW) On "The Cosby Show" with my TV family. From left to right: Sabrina Lebeauf (Sondra), Lisa Bonet (Denise), Bill Cosby (Cliff), Phylicia Rashād (Clair), Keshia Knight Pulliam (Rudy), and Tempestt Bledsoe (Vanessa).

This picture was taken of me with Rob Stone when we were making the ABC After School Special, "A Desperate Exit," 1985.

(RIGHT) My first TV movie was The Father Clements Story. *Here I am on the set with Lou Gossett, Jr., and Carroll O'Connor, 1986.*
(BELOW) Here I am presenting Anthony Quinn with a lifetime achievement award from HAMAS, 1988.

PLAYBILL

ASTOR PLACE THEATRE

(RIGHT) This is the program from my New York stage debut, Three Ways Home, *which began its run during the summer of 1988.*
(BELOW) Celebrating my high school graduation with my mom and my dad in June 1988.

or not. It really doesn't matter, and wanting to just die because, like, some guy doesn't like you is no reason to just give up.
                                        —Kimberly, 18

I attempted suicide once. I thought about cutting my wrist, or jumping off of something, but that was painful and I wanted no pain. So I did that thing with the car in the garage, like on television. They found me asleep in the car and I was saved. Not that I wanted to be or anything. Now I go to a therapist and I'm okay. My friends told me about your show because they thought it could help me to watch it. They're still afraid I might try something again, but I don't think I will.
                                        —Julie, 14

There was a line in "A Desperate Exit" which went something like "When you kill yourself you not only kill the person you are but you also kill all the people you might become." That's stayed with me. It's stayed with me, I think, because it's a reminder that the impulse toward suicide is a temporary one, and if that impulse is thwarted there are whole lifetimes out there to be built and lived and cherished. We are all here to make the most of our lives, not the least of them; suicide makes the least of them.

I think there are times when all of us don't know what to do with the rest of our lives, but it's important to remember that there will be a rest of our lives.

I read somewhere that a lot of stress and depression is created when you take too many things on, but how do you know when to stop?
                                        —Ellen

★ 145 ★

My life is really messed up and I can't cope. I have attempted suicide more times than once.
—Jessica

My parents live apart and because I can't com-municate with both of them at the same time I'm writing to you. My parents think I shouldn't have a boyfriend until I'm 17. I'm 16 now. I think they're wrong. There's this boy I know who lives near me and he tells me that my parents don't have to know about us. We really are in love, but I can't be dishonest to my parents.
—Jolene, 16

When I was preparing for "A Desperate Exit," I did a lot of research. The producers of the show gave me a lot of books and articles to read, and I studied for the role as if it were a final exam. Here, I've done the work; you can copy down my notes. (All of my information, here, comes from the American Association of Suicidology.) I learned that a successful (what an unfortunate term!) suicide is committed once every seventeen minutes; young people under the age of twenty-four kill themselves at the rate of one every one hour and thirty-seven minutes. Whites are far more likely to commit suicide than nonwhites. Suicide is the second most common cause of death among young people. Females outpace males in attempted suicides by 3 to 1, although males are successful at a rate 3.7 times greater than that of females. There are 200 attempts for every suicide among young people (the national rate is between 8 and 20 attempts). More than five million living Americans have attempted suicide at least once. Each suicide intimately affects at least six survivors, not counting friends and extended family members and teachers.

Pretty depressing numbers, and they're even more depressing when you stop to figure they could be much higher if we had any kind of consistent reporting of suicides and suicide attempts. But more important than the numbers, I also learned what to look for behind those numbers. I learned that roughly eighty percent of kids who attempt suicide make their intentions known to at least one other person, sometimes to a number of people, and sometimes in a number of ways. Clues can be left directly or indirectly. Sometimes kids give away prized possessions (like the kite my character, Charlie, gave away in "A Desperate Exit," or something like a record collection, or clothes, or a bicycle) and make other final arrangements. Sometimes kids come right out and say things like "I'm going to kill myself" or "You won't have me to worry about anymore," or sometimes their verbal threats are less obvious. Sometimes there's a major change in a kid's personality (a shy kid becomes outgoing; a friendly kid becomes withdrawn), or in a kid's behavior (an active kid becomes tired and sluggish). Sometimes kids lose their appetite or are suddenly given to wide mood swings. Sometimes kids lash out physically, fighting with friends and family members.

Most times suicidal kids are involved with drugs and alcohol. Most times suicidal kids have problems at home, and nearly ninety percent report that their families do not understand them. Most times there is an overwhelming feeling of unhappiness and hopelessness and helplessness.

Okay, so these are the danger signals. But what do you do about it if you see these signals in a friend, or even in yourself? Well, for one thing, don't be afraid to talk about it. I mean, really talk about it. If you're the one who feels suicidal, don't feel alone. Many people have felt the same way as you do at some time in their lives. What you're feeling is nothing to be ashamed of. It's important to get help, but if the idea of going to an adult with your problems is intimidating, it's okay to start with a good friend. If you don't have a friend to talk things through with, that's okay too. Many communities have suicide prevention centers and hotlines staffed by trained young people. You can talk to someone your own age who's in a good position to help; many times you'll find that the person on the other end of the phone has gone through just what you're going through now. (I've listed some numbers at the end of this book which should help you to locate the best suicide-prevention programs in your area.) If you're worried about privacy, you don't even have to give your name.

If you notice that a friend is going through a tough time don't wait for him to bring it up in conversation. The experts I talked to suggest you open the discussion, which you can do with a simple line like "Hey, how's everything going?" or "Is there anything you want to talk about?"

When people come right out and tell you they're thinking about suicide, prevention experts say you should ask them how they plan to do it, when, and whether they've taken any steps toward carrying out their plan. Think it through with them. Make them be specific. Don't be afraid that your questions will encourage them to go through with it. Actually, the people who study these things say they could have the opposite effect. Ask also about their reasons, and try to get a good sense of what they're thinking, how they're feeling, how much thought they've put into it.

A lot of times it's a good idea to let on that you've had some of the same feelings, and you've learned that you can work through these feelings. As I said earlier, studies show that suicidal intentions come and go; it's only because young people are so impulsive and act so quickly on their impulses that they don't stick around long enough to realize that their desperate situation is only temporary. They don't give themselves a chance to get some perspective on the situation. So you see how it's important to act quickly.

The thing you don't want to do is end the discussion

too soon. The people I talked to say you should keep your friend talking for as long as he's comfortable, not dismiss him early on with lines like "What are you talking about?" or "You're so much better off than most people." If you do that, you're sending signals that you're not really willing to listen and to help, and that you don't really understand; you're shutting him off and in shutting him off you reinforce his feelings of hopelessness and isolation. Keep the conversation going the way you'd talk about any other topic with any other friend.

Next, try to convince your friend to talk to someone else, someone older, preferably someone in a position to offer real help. If a parent is part of the problem, there are other adults to turn to: a relative, a teacher, a counselor, a doctor, a clergyman. Suggest he go to a suicide-prevention center and offer to go along for support. If he won't go, go behind his back and seek help on his behalf, or at the very least, go alone to make sure you've done everything you could and that you haven't sent any of the wrong signals. Don't worry about being a snitch or betraying a confidence. In this case the ends justify the means. The most important thing is to get your friend some kind of help, and sometimes that might mean you have to go out and get help for him. You have to get counseling on your counseling.

Remember, we all have good times and bad times. The bad times get better. The good times come back. Remember also, there are people who can help and there are people who want to help.

Lately I've been putting myself down or getting really depressed about things people say about me or sometimes over stupid things like guys. I have thought about suicide lots of times but I couldn't bring myself to really killing myself. Usually I talk to friends about it. A lot of my friends tell me they think about it but never try it. Sometimes we talk about different ways to do it.

—Nicole, 14

My dad has a girlfriend and he's hardly ever at home, so that means I'm alone ninety-five percent of the time. My life right now isn't perfect at all. And there are times it can get very frightening and I need someone to talk to and I have no one. I keep reaching out to touch but there's nothing there. I think a lot. You have to when you don't have anyone to talk to. But I guess I do because it's me. I like to sit in dark rooms staring out of a window, wondering what else is the world doing.

—Tanya, 18

Why do so many teenagers commit suicide? It is a waste of life. Once you are dead there is no coming back. Remember, a few years ago, there was a mass suicide? And then there were two or three more the next week. It seemed like a disease you'd hear about on the news. Now whenever I have a problem, I try to put it in perspective. It works. No more problem.

—Ronald, 17

I remember when I first heard the news about that group of friends who got together and made a suicide pact. It happened in New Jersey a few years ago. Me and my friends talked about it for days after it happened. It didn't make any sense to us. I still can't understand it. I mean, here were four kids, each of them obviously close enough to three other people to talk about dying together, so why is it that they couldn't find some other way out of their problems? Why is it that they couldn't find some way to go on living together? It just didn't make sense.

That's why it's so important to look out for clues. I can't believe that four kids in the same community plotted a joint suicide without leaving some really clear signs about what they were up to.

Pay attention.

Everyone thinks about suicide sometimes. I know I have. We don't realize that ending our lives will not solve anything, but just add to the problems of those we love. I know that if I attempted suicide, my parents and friends would go crazy figuring out where "they" went wrong. Death doesn't solve anything. There is always someone, somewhere, willing to listen to your feelings.

—Peter, 16

Hi. I'm 17, and at one point I considered killing myself. I have several friends who have had similar feelings, and one in particular that tried and failed, and that little incident has ruined his life. Some people claim nobody could understand what they are going through, but ten to one someone in this world has gone through the same experience, and lived through it. And another thing, there is always someone worse off than you are.

—Amy, 17

Never mind what you read about teenage suicide. I think it's slowing down. They teach you about it in schools, and on television, and kids know how dangerous it can be.

—Adam, 13

It's dumb to try suicide, because it can end your life in more ways than one. Colleges don't need students who are just wasting their time, and employers do not want suicidal employees. An act like this at such a young age will follow you around for life.

—*Cheryl, 15*

I am troubled by these last two letters, because they suggest to me that some kids don't make the connection that suicide is something more than some kind of cry for help. They seem to separate the act of suicide from actually dying. It's two different things to them. Think about it: "An act like this will follow you around for life." "Kids know how dangerous it can be." There's something wrong with that kind of mind-set, and I get a lot of letters that indicate the same kind of attitude. Read into it and you see a kid who looks at suicide as just a form of expression, a release, a way to let your friends and family know that you're not happy or that you're in trouble. It's a cry for help, is what it is to them, nothing more, but too many kids don't put it together that it's a cry for help that will not be heard.

Look back at the statistics I rattled off earlier and you'll see that two hundred young people try to kill themselves for every one that succeeds. Two hundred to one! We've got to worry about every one of those two hundred, but it's that one person who completes what he set out to do that we should worry about the most. You have to realize that most kids who try to kill themselves don't really want to die: they shoot to miss. They may want to commit suicide, but they don't want to die, not really, and sometimes a kid who succeeds in killing himself succeeds only by accident. We've all got to pay better attention so that one kid in two hundred doesn't attempt suicide and *accidentally* succeed.

I need somebody to talk to when I'm down, under the weather, and that's why I write to you. It helps the pain go away. Writing to you (I also write to Janet Jackson, I hope you don't mind) makes me think about a lot of things. I know when I go back to school everybody is going to talk about me and this stupid new haircut I got. It really looks stupid. But I don't care as long as I know I got you. I can write to you and cry. I know that you won't probably read this, but I don't care. Like I said, it helps me a lot.

—Charlotte, 15

Charlotte, I'm glad you wrote, I did read your letter, and I do care. I just wish, for all of you who reached out, that I could do more. Just remember that there are lots of people in your own communities who can do more, lots more. Find them. Talk to them.

12

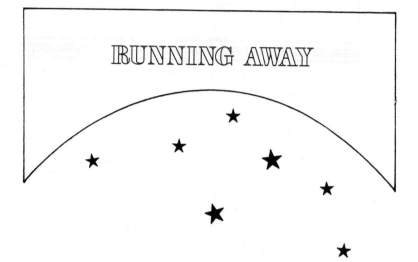

RUNNING AWAY

NOTES ON LEAVING HOME

My parents are divorced and I have a lot of problems. I have also tried running away and killing myself. I was lucky, someone was there to help me. Now I'm home and things are starting to be okay again. Some others may not be so lucky.

—Randi, 16

There is this place near the railroad tracks where I live, it has this big boulder and underneath the overhang I have some old cushions and fruit crates to use as stools. I go there some-

times when I need to be away from my family.
I'm by myself there. They yell a lot, my parents.
                                        —Michael, 12

I am in a shelter for runaways. It's an okay
place, but there's no one to talk to. We watch
your show in the lounge on Thursday nights
and I thought, you know, maybe I could talk to
you. There are counselors here and everything,
but I don't trust them or the other girls enough
to talk to them. You can't trust people here.
                                        —Lacey, 14

Now, there are runaways, and then there are runaways. When I was a little kid, running away meant disappearing to a friend's house, or a relative's, for a few hours. It meant grabbing a sleeping bag and hiding out in the woods. It was a way to get out some aggression and exert some authority and get some space. It was also a way to act out against your parents. It still means the same things to a lot of kids, but now it also means a whole lot more. Now it sometimes means a life alone, on the streets, in trouble, with nowhere to turn.

Actually, it probably meant all the same things then; it's just that I was too young to notice.

I look at the numbers now and they're scary. The best estimates put the numbers at between 1.5 and 2 million kids each year who run away from home. Two million kids! Now, to be fair, that's a pretty generous estimate. The people at The National Network of Runaway and Youth Services in Washington, D.C., tell me it includes all those kids who cooled off at Grandma's house with some milk and cookies, and all those who hid out in their parents' basement for a few hours.

But it also includes all the other kids who were seeking a very serious and very permanent escape from very serious family problems. Nearly half of all kids who run away from home are being physically or sexually abused. Most are emotionally abused. Almost all are running away from something, whether it's their parents' crumbling marriage, or their parents' drinking problems or financial concerns, or whatever. A lot of these kids eventually return home and set about mending the broken family relationships they've left behind, that's true, but a lot of them wind up on the street, or in temporary shelters or foster homes. Too many of them never return home and too many others don't have a home to go back to.

The National Network reports there are about one million runaway kids, with a median age of fifteen, currently on the streets. Roughly seventy percent of those kids are white; about twenty percent are black. Most are from middle-class families, or upper-middle-class families. Among that group, there is an unusually high incidence of malnutrition, venereal disease, and suicide. An alarming percentage is at risk of contracting AIDS.

There's a misconception out there that runaway kids are "bad" kids, that they're out only for a good time or a high adventure. That's absolutely not true. Kids who run away from home and put their safety at risk are not out for a fling, they're not out to be free of parental restrictions, they're not out for a good time. They are running away from a problem, or a series of problems, they don't know how to handle and this is the best way they can come up with to cope. This is not high adventure we're talking about here; what we're seeing is self-preservation and a whole lot of sadness.

I don't hear from a lot of these kids, but I do hear from a few.

The only thing to do was to just go away. I heard from my mom once, they have this message board on the hotline I sometimes call, but I don't want to talk to or see my father ever

again. If she moves out I'll go with her, but I doubt that will happen. She won't ever move out.
                                   —Brenda, 14

When my dad drinks he breaks things and yells. I have a cut lip from where he hit me once. It was bad. The agency where I'm at says I should have had stitches put in for it.
                                   —Matthew, 16

My father used to rape my older sister, and she told me about this place to go to so he wouldn't do me. She was crying, but I went to this place she told me about and they took me in and now I'm okay. My father's getting help and soon I'm going back home. My mother doesn't live with us.
                                   —Cleo, 13

The serious runaways, then, have to be my deepest concern in a chapter like this. I can't help them, not really, but I can listen to them. I can talk about them. Maybe that will help.

Let me get back to the numbers. In New York, for example, state agencies and shelters handle twenty-three thousand runaway cases each year, according to the folks at New York City's Covenant House. If you multiplied that out by fifty states, you'd top one million cases, but New York comes in at the high end of runaway statistics; in most states the numbers are far, far smaller. Keep in mind, there's a myth that runaway kids gravitate to the big cities, but research shows that's just a myth. In New York State, ninety percent of all runaway kids travel less than ten miles from home. I think that number surprises a lot of people. The programs are spread pretty evenly across the state, so city kids do not dominate the numbers.

The national percentages are similar. What this tells us is that kids stay close to home when they run away, and maybe what that tells us is that they don't want to leave as much as they feel they have to. Most times they're leaving behind a disintegrating family situation, but they're not running away from their friends, from their school, or from their community. They have a support network already in place, and they tend to rely on that network when they leave home. These kids are not out to put themselves at risk; that's why they tend to go where they are known, where they know they'll be safe. They feel safe in their community. They don't feel safe at home.

Sure, kids still hop on buses and head for New York or Los Angeles or Las Vegas, but those are just the kids they make movies of the week about. According to the numbers, the real problem, the more prevalent problem, stays close to home. Runaway kids are looking to get away from home; they don't need to get far.

It's funny, all I did was go in the backyard, and they called the police and everything, and I was watching the whole time. It was for like a few hours and they didn't even know I was there.
—Greg, 14

I made some calls on this one and what I found out is that a lot of runaway kids tend to blame themselves for their bad situations at home. They think it's up to them to help their father keep his job, or to stay away from drugs or alcohol; they think it's up to them to put their parents' marriage back together. But we've got to tell ourselves, and our kids, that you can't parent your parents. It's not your job; it's your parents' job. If you're being abused, you can't blame yourself for another person's victimization of you. It's absolutely not your fault.

That's an easy message to send, but I'm sure it's not so easy to hear.

My friend, she got into this trouble when she went to New York. Her parents, they didn't know about her going to New York and when they found her she was all beat up and working for a guy who was like a pimp.
—*Selina, 14*

Sometimes I'd walk up and down the streets of this fancy neighborhood and I'd look in the windows of the nice houses and watch the nice families having dinner. I wish mine could be like that. One time someone's dog heard me crying in their bushes and I had to get out of there pretty quick.
—*Colette, 15*

I used to ask people on the streets for money, and I'd get enough to eat. Usually I'd buy bread and lettuce because it was cheap. I knew kids who would pick out of garbage bags, but I couldn't do that. Now I'm in this place getting help. We watch your show in the community room.
—*Randy, 14*

I heard about this thing they do on the buses where if you're running away and change your mind and want to go home they'll let you go home for free. That's good because you don't always have the money you need.
—*Tracy, 15*

What Tracy's referring to is a wonderful program set up by Greyhound and Trailways called Operation: Home Free. It's good public relations—the bus companies will provide a one-way ticket home to runaway kids under certain circumstances—and it's good for the kids on the street to know such a program exists. (And they are aware of it, if my letters and the calls to the runaway hotline numbers are any indication.) It's a nice safety net. The thing is, as the statistics indicate, most kids don't run far enough away from home to put such a program to its fullest use.

But the bus companies are onto something. Wouldn't it be wonderful if other corporate sponsors could follow the bus companies' lead and institute other efforts appropriate to their specific service or business? A hotel chain could offer temporary safe housing, a fast-food franchise could offer free meals, a long-distance telephone service could offer free phone calls home. A medical insurance group could offer emergency medical care.

The thing that surprises me, in the letters and in my talks with experts, is that runaway kids are very much aware of all goods and services available to them. They know how the system works and they know how to work the system. What they don't know is how to take care of their most basic needs. They need as many safety nets as we can give them.

My brother and me packed some stuff and went into the woods but a neighbor who lives near the woods where we went called my house and told them where we were and not to worry.
—Peter, 11

One time I ran away but it was just to my friend's house. I took the quarters we use for the laundry, but his mom wouldn't let him come with me and she called my mom to come get me.
—Cory, 9

My brother runned away from our house because he was punished about something he did. He went to his high school and lived there for two days over vacation. He showered in the

locker room and found stuff to eat in the cafete-
ria. The custodians sell drugs to his friends so
they left him alone.

—*Rianna, 12*

Of course, there is a light side to this dark problem.
Or maybe it's better to say a soft side to a hard problem.
To be honest, most of my letters on running away are from
good kids, from good families, kids who would never think
to put themselves in any kind of jeopardy, kids with loving
and caring parents. They run away because their folks
won't let them stay out past midnight on Saturday nights,
or because they can't borrow the car when they want to.
They run away for a day or two, even for an hour or two,
and they don't run far. When we talk about runaway kids,
we usually mean the kids running away from big problems, but there are a whole lot of kids out there looking to
run away from much smaller dilemmas.

As a little kid, I'd lie awake in bed sometimes and
think about running away whenever things didn't go the
way I wanted. I think every kid does. I never could get
very far, either in my head or in actuality, because my
mother slept in the living room, and I'd have to get past
her to get past the door, but it did cross my mind a time
or two. I remember one time—I must have been in the
second grade—I was learning to write in cursive, and
every time I made a mistake my mom would hit me with
this cloth slipper she had. It didn't hurt or anything; it was
just a way of teaching me to concentrate. But what it did
hurt was my pride. She kept doing it to me, over and over,
until I got the whole thing right. I remember thinking,
"I'm going to run away." I made this whole plan in my
head. I even cried myself to sleep that night, thinking of
the letter I would leave for my mother (in script, of course):
"Don't bother looking for me because you're never going
to find me and I'm never coming home." Stuff like that.
Eventually I fell asleep, and by the time I woke up in the

morning I had pretty much forgotten what I was mad about.

Besides, I was always pretty realistic about things. I knew that if I ran away, there was no place I could go where no one would call my mother. How was I going to eat? And watch television? (I sure had my priorities straight when I was a little kid.)

Believe it or not, we even did an episode about this on "The Cosby Show." (Man, we've got episodes for everything on that show!) On this one, Rudy ran away because she was all frustrated about being only five years old and unable to do the same "big people" things as everyone else in her family. Actually, she didn't run away so much as she went and hid in this box in the backyard, but the point was the same: she needed to kick up some dust to let her folks know she was upset, and she also needed some privacy and some time to cool off. I guess the reason she didn't run any farther than her own backyard was that the producers didn't want to send the wrong signals to other kids watching the show. The "right" signal they sent was, it's okay to go and be by yourself once in a while, even if you're only five years old. Rudy needed her privacy, and the only place she could find to get it was in a box in her yard. Lots of kids have these secret hiding places, or clubhouses, or whatever, where they go to sort things out in their head. Adults have them too, so why shouldn't we? Sometimes even a little kid needs to put some distance on a situation.

My friend was in his attic for the whole night and no one even knew he was gone. Weird, huh?
—Marlene, 13

We read these books in school, books like Huckleberry Finn, and they make running away sound like fun. Do you think this is what they had in mind?
—Terence, 15

Please, if you could, please call my mom and dad for me and tell them my terms. I need a new stereo and/or new Nike basketball shoes, or else they can just forget about me.
—Noah, 16

What I do when I need to be alone is I go ride my bicycle. I just go, I don't think about where I'm going. My dad says when he drives his car it helps him clear his head up, and it helps him sort through his problems and be by himself. That's what bike riding does for me too.
—Christopher, 14

The experts I talked to say we need some more peer counseling programs to help runaway kids. Makes sense to me: kids talk to other kids first, or at least they're most willing to talk to other kids. Let's train our children in schools to help counsel and support their peers, on this issue and on others. There are a bunch of successful programs around the country on which to base our efforts. Help us to help ourselves.

Some basic advice to kids who feel themselves inching toward the door: talk to someone before you do anything that might threaten your health or your safety. If your problem is with one parent, talk to the other (if there is an other); if your problem is with both parents, try to sit them down and make your feelings known. If that seems impossible, talk to someone outside the immediate family. Often an aunt or an uncle or a grandparent can intervene on your behalf. Talk to an older brother or sister. Talk to your friends. Talk to your teachers or your guidance counselors at school. Think things through. Call one of the toll-free numbers listed at the end of the book and see about getting some direct and targeted help in your community.

Above all, if you are in any real and present danger, leave. If you feel threatened in any way, physically or emotionally, leave. Your first obligation is to yourself and to your safety. You can worry about working on your family problems later.

Parents, pay attention to your kids. The same warning signals described in the discussion of suicide also apply here. Don't be quick to dismiss their concerns. Look at your own behavior honestly and from your child's perspective. Most times you can keep a kid at home if you spend time with him, and if you listen.

If you notice that your child is missing, act quickly. A lot of times the local police departments won't act on a missing persons report until that person has been gone for twenty-four hours, but get your call into them as soon as you're aware something's wrong. Most local police will also give your child's name and description to the FBI's National Crime Information Center. If they won't do it, do it yourself. This will alert authorities outside your immediate area. Talk to your kid's friends to find out where he was last seen, and with whom. See if anyone has any ideas where he might be. Call the toll-free hotline numbers and ask if your child has left a message. Leave one for him.

Remember, running away doesn't mean you want to go off and live by yourself on Gilligan's Island. It means you want your situation at home to improve, or you want a way out of your situation at home. Most times there are other ways out of that situation without your having to leave home.

13

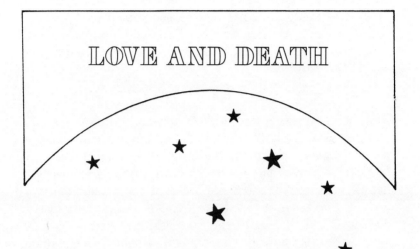

LOVE AND DEATH

NOTES ON DEALING WITH LOSS AND ILLNESS

We went to visit my grandmother in the hospital and the woman in the bed next to her had these tubes in her nose, sticking out. Also, my grandmother smelled funny but I had to kiss her anyway. My dad said so.

—Alexa, 11

Here's a poem I wrote about when my sister died. It doesn't rhyme, but it tells how I feel. "Her room is empty now/I like to sleep in her bed and dream her dreams for her/I think I'll

always miss her." I'm going to make it longer and send it in for the school paper.
—*Corinne, 15*

My best friend was killed in a car accident last year. I could talk to her about anything, then she was just gone and that really hurt me up inside. Now I am still scared to get close to another person.
—*Helene, 16*

Dealing with death and serious illness is almost always uncharted territory for kids, and if my mail is any measure it's not a place they often get through unchanged. Hospitals and funerals have a way of leaving their marks on people of all ages, and I see some of these marks in my letters. I've been over a few of these rough spots in my own life, and I'll get to them a little bit later on in this chapter, but for now let's just look a little bit at what some of these kids are going through when they open up to me about the death of a parent or a sibling or a friend.

I know I'm a sounding board for a lot of kids about a lot of things—I've said that before—but it's these letters, the ones which start to get at the pain of loss or the fear of loss, that get me thinking how isolated and lonely and vulnerable we are sometimes left by the people we love. Death is a tough thing to talk about, and I guess it's just a little less tough to write about. I don't know; maybe kids feel better in getting some things off their chest, and the easiest and least threatening way to do that is to write to someone like me, someone who can't pass judgment on how lonely or vulnerable they're feeling, someone who won't ask them to say or feel anything they don't want to say or feel. I can't hurt them in any way; they can open up to me and spill their guts on paper, and they don't have to worry that any of it will come back to haunt them.

I'm an easy ear.

I hear from kids worrying through an uncle's bout with cancer, and I hear from kids whose dads are going through open heart surgery. A lot of times I hear from a kid who's just lost a parent or a sibling or a very special friend; they write to tell me how different they feel, after what they've just been through, and they write to tell me how the other kids treat them differently at school, how sometimes their teachers even reinforce those feelings by singling them out with special treatment.

Read over my shoulder for a bit:

My grandfather is dying. He has been in the hospital something like five times in the last four months. Every time I look at him I just want to cry. I just can't adjust to losing him and him being in pain. Sometimes I wish he could pass away in the night without any pain.
—Beth Anne, 15

I'm in the hospital now. I broke both my legs in a car crash. It was pretty neat, and I don't remember if it hurt. I remember the ambulance, a little bit. I'm writing lots of letters to people now because there's not much to do. My mother visits, but my dad has to work and my brothers are in school. Tomorrow I'm learning how to use crutches.
—Wayne, 15

What my brother has is water on the lung. It's not so very rare. They say maybe he could die from it but probably not. I don't know what to do. He's seeing lots of doctors.
—Jokala, 13

My cousin has AIDS, and he's got it pretty bad. He's in and out of the hospital. Now he's in. We don't go see him, because my mom's worried about our seeing him. We call him on the phone, except when it's my turn I never know what to say.

—Geoffrey, 13

I'm terrible when it comes to hospitals. It's one of my weak spots. For some reason, me and hospitals don't get along. I want to be there for my friends, or for my family, or for whoever it is I'm visiting, but I just freeze up in that kind of setting. I get all tense and nervous and sweaty-palmed when I'm going to visit someone, and I do everything I can to avoid going. I know it's immature of me, but I still have trouble with it.

I am working on myself, though, and I think I'm getting better at it. It's my problem, and it's not fair of me to deny the love and support friends or family members need simply because I'm made a little bit uncomfortable by their hospitalization. It's something I have to get past, and even if it's slow going right now I'm determined to get there.

You know, it's funny, Theo's got something of the same problem. Or at least he had. We did an episode on the show about a friend of Theo's who was in the hospital for cancer. Theo felt a lot of what I would feel in the same situation. He didn't want to go visit his friend in the hospital because he didn't think he could handle the way his friend was going to be. He had this image of what it would be like to have cancer, and he couldn't reconcile himself with that image as it related to his friend. He liked his friend just the way he was—healthy, normal, active. He liked it that his friend was just like him. All of his other friends were back and forth to the hospital all the time, and they were saying to Theo, "Listen, this is your buddy, this is your pal, he's asking about you, you've got to go see him."

He'd keep coming up with some excuse or other, and he stayed away.

★ 168 ★

Eventually Theo decided to go, and when he got there he was going through a lot of what I always go through. He didn't know how to act around his friend; he was worried that he might say or do the wrong thing. There was even a scene where he was pacing outside the door to his friend's room, putting off going inside. He was so unsure of himself, the nurse finally had to coax him through the door.

When he went into the room he wasn't much better. He was stiff and uneasy around his friend and his attempts at small talk were, well, pretty small: "Nice weather we're having," stuff like that. His friend was telling him to treat him just as if they were at school, or just as if they were at home, to forget that he was in a hospital room with someone suffering from cancer, but Theo's thing was, how can he forget he was in a hospital room with someone suffering from cancer? He was having a lot of trouble. It was the friend who finally put Theo at ease, and not the other way around. It should have been the other way around. By the end of the show, Theo relaxed a little bit, enough so he was joking and horsing around with his friend just as he would outside the hospital. They were even playing basketball with some rolled-up socks, but it took a good long while to get there.

The lesson of this show (there's always a lesson, right?) is that your friends are no different simply because they're sick. In fact, they need you to remind them they're no different simply because they're sick. They need you to treat them the same way you've always treated them, and they need you to be honest and open and up-front with them. The other lesson, the hidden lesson, is that life goes on. You can be holed up in the hospital with the worst kind of cancer, or you can be in traction with two broken legs, and your friends will still be going to school, and to basketball games, and to parties. There'll still be homework you're not doing. Theo learned how important it is to keep your friends plugged into the day-to-day routines they've

★ 169 ★

put on hold during an illness. They need to feel a part of things.

Theo gave it his best shot and got over something that was in the way of his being a better person. I'm trying to do the same. Each year I appear on the Children's Miracle Network Telethon, which is sponsored by the Osmond Foundation on behalf of children's hospitals around the country. (Last year we generated nearly $40 million in donations!) As a part of my involvement, I also travel around the country, visiting children's hospitals, trying to help out wherever I can. It's funny, but I look forward to these visits, even if hospitals aren't the easiest environment for me. The cool thing about it is that my being there makes these children feel good; it makes a difference, and that's the important thing. It makes me feel good to know I make them feel good. It's amazing: a lot of the kids I visit are terminally ill, and yet they seem to be the happiest kids I come across. They don't hold a grudge against the world, the way you'd think; they don't seem to be bitter at all; and when I'm with them their smiles just light up the rest of my world.

Sometimes I wonder why I have such trouble visiting my own friends or relatives, and why it's so easy, even pleasant, to visit perfect strangers. Of course I know it's different when there's a personal attachment, but then I recognize that as soon as I walk into each kid's room there's a personal attachment. So it's not only that. I don't know what it is, but I'm determined to find out. If Theo can get over his fear of hospitals, then so can I. It won't be so easy for me—he's got better writers than I do, for one thing—and it will probably take more time than twenty-three minutes plus commercials, but I'm working on it.

The other thing I'm working on is offering my condolences. It's a fact of growing up that sooner or later you're going to be asked to help a friend suffer through the loss of a loved one. It's a time, and a task, you may have some trouble with, but you've just got to work your way through it. I've had friends who've lost parents or siblings, and I've tried to be there for them. I hope I was some kind of help, but I'm not entirely sure that I was. I think so. I knew how hard it was on them, and I felt for what they were going through, believe me, but I was having considerable troubles of my own. I don't think people pay enough attention to how hard it is on those doing the consoling. I don't mean to sound callous or insensitive, so don't misunderstand me. I only mean to offer credit, and support, to those of us who are called on to give our support to our friends in need, and feel hopelessly ill-equipped for the task. If you think about it, the odds are that we'll be called on to offer our love and support a lot more frequently than we'll need some for ourselves.

Helping someone through a devastating loss is not easy, and it's not something you can prepare for either. The lessons learned in the "Cosby" episode, in the hospital, also apply here, with modification. Treat your friend as an equal; don't put him on any kind of sensitive pedestal for too long. Let him know that you're there for him and that you care about him and that you want to help make it easy for him to get back to business as usual. Two words of advice: be yourself. Ten more (not including parentheses): if you don't know how to help, ask for guidance (a friend, a parent, a teacher).

> *I don't know how to handle my dad's death. It's been three years now, and every time the anniversary comes around it's so depressing. I have a brother and a sister, but they're older, and it's so unfair because they got to grow up with him being around and I didn't. I was only seven.*
> *—Shana, 10*

*Both of my parents are deceased. They died
when I was little. I really envy people who have
parents. I miss mine very much.*
                                    —*Stephanie, 14*

*One year I got home from a trip and there was
terrible news when I got there. My father had
died. I was shocked and lost control and I don't
remember what I did, but I remember feeling
tremendous guilt, because I was away on a trip
for school when he died. I feel like I should have
been there.*
                                    —*Lisa, 16*

I've watched both of my parents lose one of their
parents, and I think in both cases the way I responded
depended on the way they reacted to the news. My
mother's father passed away as I was writing this book.
He'd been in a hospital for several years with Alzheimer's
disease, and I'd seen him less and less as his condition got
worse and worse. Part of that had to do with me and my
thing about hospitals, part of it was that he was in Los
Angeles and me and my mom were in New York, but
mostly it was because my visits would make no kind of
impact on my grandfather. He didn't know that I was
there, and my being there was no kind of comfort to him,
and after a while it just became easier for me to stay away.
I feel bad about that now. My mother went through a little
bit of the same thing. She also saw him less and less. Now,
when I think of him, I remember him the way he was when
I was five or six or seven, the way he was before he was
hospitalized. That's the way I want to remember him.

When he died it was like hearing the other shoe drop.
In the backs of our heads, I guess we were expecting the
news, but I don't think we were really prepared for it. No
matter how much of a reality death is, I don't think it's
something you can ever prepare for, not fully. There was

a part of him, I think, that we buried long before he died, but there was a part of him also that was still very much alive.

I took a leave from "The Cosby Show" to fly out for the funeral. Now, I'm as bad with funerals as I am with hospitals, but for this one I put aside my fears and uncertainties and went ahead. Mostly I went to be there for my mother, to lend her some support. We both cried, she for her father and me for my mother, but for the most part she was strong about it, and I took my cue from her. For myself, I didn't feel a tremendous sense of loss or anything like that, I guess because I hadn't had much of a relationship with my grandfather for ten years or so. For him, I could feel only relief that he was free finally from his suffering.

I was much younger when my dad's mother died. I was seven years old. I don't remember much about that time, but what I do remember is that she was in the hospital for about a week, and my dad would go to see her every day. One day he got there and she had died. He had just missed her. Looking back, I realize that must have been awful tough for him to take. Me and my mom were living in Los Angeles by then, and when she told me there were tears in her eyes. She had been very close to my grandmother. She was crying and so I thought I should be crying too. When I went to the funeral I cried some more. I remember thinking that everybody else was crying, and I thought it must be that crying is the thing to do at funerals.

That was the first time I ever lost someone close to me, and I don't know how much of what happened, or what it meant, actually sunk in for me. It registered that my grandmother was gone, and that I would never see her again. I knew a little bit about what death meant, but really only enough to understand how her death would affect me. I processed the news in terms of not being able to see her again, and I cried about it because I saw my parents crying about it.

It's always been interesting to me exactly how much little kids are able to understand about life and death. At that point I was only able to understand very little. I don't know exactly when that changed for me, but it changes for all of us at some point.

Now that I have a little perspective on what my father went through, I'm able to feel for his loss all the more. Sure, I miss my grandmother, and my grandfather, but mostly what I feel now that they're gone is this tremendous sadness for my folks, for what they're missing.

I don't know how I'd handle losing my mom or dad. It's not something I like to think about, but for a lot of kids out there, life without a parent is a part of their reality.

Everybody says I look like my Daddy. He was a engineer before he died. He made lots of money. I was 10 when he died. I want to be an engineer too and take care of my mother and sisters.
—Andrew, 11

My mother was killed when I was a baby. When I first heard it I wasn't supposed to have heard it. I wasn't supposed to know until I was older, but I found out when I was about ten. Back then I could not cry, but now I can.
—Barbara, 16

Both my parents are dead, my mother since I was six, my father since last year. We're split up, me and my brothers and sisters. I'm with my baby sister at my aunt's, and my two brothers are with my grandmother in New York, and my older sister is away at college. We try to still be a family but it's hard.
—Heidi, 14

There's no way to prepare for the sudden death of a parent. It can be one of the most emotional and frightening crises in the life of a child, and it can forever change the course of a kid's future development. His world will be turned upside down, and it will be no easy task to set it right again.

Losing a mother or a father can be devastating. I haven't yet come across any "right" way of dealing with it. Losing someone else you love, outside your immediate family, isn't any easier.

Two years ago my uncle died. We had fun to-gether, but now he's not here to have fun with and I don't know what to do. Should I be glad he doesn't have to suffer (he was sick), or what should I feel?

—Nathan, 15

A very close relative of mine has recently com-mitted suicide. It left me feeling so awful and helpless.

—Marjorie, 16

There was this car accident at my school and two kids from my school were killed, and one person in the other car, except the kid who was driving is okay and back at school already. He wasn't hurt at all, and no one knows what to say to him.

—Adam, 15

My friends are different to me since my baby brother died. He had leukemia and he was in remission from it for a while but then he got bad again and died. He was just seven, going on eight. Now my friends are all weird to me, like they think I'm gonna burst out crying all the time.

—*Robin, 14*

I did a lot of reading before I put my thoughts on paper here, and what I learned was that children have to be eased into an understanding of death. It's a gradual process. Many psychologists suggest introducing the concept gently and indirectly, like in a conversation about plants and flowers. Ideally the subject will come up before the child loses someone close to him.

A lot of kids first learn about death through the loss of a pet, and sometimes that makes the concept easier to understand. On "The Cosby Show" we did an episode where Rudy's goldfish died (I think every long-running family sitcom eventually does an episode about dead goldfish), and it was all about how Rudy learned to accept her loss. We had the standard sitcom funeral in the family bathroom, complete with eulogy and Last Rites, and by the time the show ended Rudy was through with her mourning. She was onto something else.

What that show tells us, also, is that life goes on. We all have different ways of dealing with our grief, ranging from a five-year-old little girl who is merely distracted from it, like Rudy, on up to our most mature adults, who process their grief and put it into a form that they're able to look at and deal with and then move on. What I've found is that even our experts on grief and its effect on children are divided on what kids are able to understand and respond to about death, and at what age, and so maybe the best thing to do is see what works best for you and your family.

I think one of the most important things I learned in my reading is that it's okay to cry. All the time you hear people say things like "Be brave, don't cry," and yet I couldn't find one good reason for holding back tears. Not one. If you ask me, all these well-meaning older relatives are encouraging this unemotional behavior just to make their job of consoling that much easier. There's no reason not to cry. In fact, there's every reason to cry. Let it go. Tears can be a tremendous relief, an unburdening. They won't change the situation any, that's for sure, but there's no reason to stop them if they feel like coming. They may make you feel better, even if it's just for a little while.

Incidentally, the flip side also holds. Don't feel obligated to cry. There's nothing wrong with you if the emotions you're feeling don't lead to tears. If the tears don't come, don't force them. It doesn't mean you didn't love the person who died enough, or as much as everyone else.

Parents, help your kids to remember the good things and the bad things about the person who died. A careful review with your child of his history with the deceased is a good way to assist in the mourning process, and a good way to help your child sort through his feelings. Tell him it's okay to feel two ways about a person, that there can be bad feelings mixed in with the good and that there's no reason to feel guilty for thinking about the bad feelings. Experts say this kind of emotional review is a good way to begin your child's task of getting on with the rest of his life.

That's the key, getting on. Whether you've lost a good friend, a parent, a brother or sister, or anybody else you care deeply about, the only way to pick up the pieces is one at a time.

14

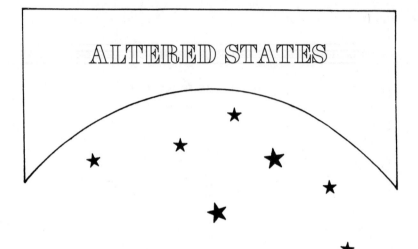

NOTES ON DRUG AND ALCOHOL ABUSE

I am scared to death about drugs, ever since I was little. I am sure, pretty sure, that if someone asked me to do drugs I can say no, but I worry that someone may force them on me.
—Gabrielle, 15

I have some friends that do drugs and I do them because they do.
—Jimmy, 17

Most drugs are in many different colors. For little kids it's hard because they think it's candy. It is also hard for teens and pre-teens.

—Jessica, 11

Do you have any advice on how to just say no? Please, I need some.

—Alan, 14

Before we get going here, let me sneak in a few words about something that's been bothering me, on and off, for the past few years:

So much has been said and written about drug and alcohol abuse among our young people that I'm almost reluctant to add to the chorus. I mean, I know I've added to the chorus before, and I'm sure I will again, talking in schools and at rallies, making public service commercials, and whatever, but I think it's time we changed the song, at least a little bit. We could even just add a few more verses.

Here's what I mean: kids are a lot smarter than the people behind these campaigns give us credit for. I'm all for the awareness these campaigns have generated—that's terrific—but kids have to look someplace else beyond the campaigns for solutions. "Just Say No!" may work in theory, but it doesn't always cut it in practice.

Look, I get behind all of these "Just Say No!" campaigns because they're the best we've got and it's the least I can do, but a part of me holds back. I can't get all the way behind them because I think they're missing something. Exactly what they're missing I'm not sure, but something's not there that should be there.

How can you just say no? Turning away from drugs is not about just saying no. It's harder than that. There's a lot of other stuff going on. You have to realize that when you're in high school everything you do, or don't do, follows you around the hallways of your school for as long as you're there. It becomes as much a part of who you are as your name. People have something to say about everything and everyone. There's more to getting through growing up than just saying no. There's everything that goes along with just saying no.

Don't misunderstand me, the campaign has done a wonderful job of heightening awareness among kids about the dangers of drug abuse, but the line itself—"Just Say No"—is in danger of becoming a slogan. It's nearly there, and the more of a slogan it becomes, the more I think we lose the meaning behind it. The campaign is built on the idea that you're saying no once, but in reality kids who say no are saying no every minute of every hour of every day. We've got to find a way to account for that, and to help kids with that.

Okay, I've said my bit. Now, let's get into what some other kids have to say.

> *Could you ask your producer to create an episode where a kid who uses drugs is helped by you to say no? Also, please go to more schools and talk about this.*
>
> *—Dillon, 14*

> *It seems like children under twelve are taking drugs. It's always a problem with parents, or school isn't going right for them. I don't understand it.*
>
> *—Arlene*

> *My friends say that I am a square because I won't smoke pot with them. I make up excuses not to go to parties because they make fun of me.*
>
> *—Miriam, 18*

*At one time drugs were the cool and "in" thing
to do, but now it all seems so stupid.*
—Nancy, 17

I'm not going to bog you down with statistics here, the
way I did in some other chapters. The numbers are there,
and believe me, they're frightening. It's just that when it
comes to drug use and abuse, the numbers mean less to me
than the climate. And the climate, I'm happy to report, is
changing, even if it's only changing slowly.

There is a shift taking place in the attitudes kids bring
to drugs. It's funny, because most of us, or at least a lot
of us, are growing up with parents who spent their high
school and college days with a beer in one hand and a joint
in the other. It wasn't even a generation ago when there
was this whole casual attitude about drug use. Even five
years ago you'd find basically good kids, in basically good
neighborhoods, at basically good high schools, drinking or
getting high between classes. You still find that in some
schools that's true, but a lot's changed in five years.

One thing that hasn't changed, though, is the parents.
Our parents (and I don't mean my parents here, just parents in general) are telling us not to drink or get high, and
then they turn around and get drunk or stoned. It's hard
for kids to reconcile one message with the other.

We need to get our parents on the same side of the
fence if we're gonna get moving on this thing.

*My mother and father have company over and
they drink and have a good, loud time. I know
for a fact that some of them get high. I saw. And
then they drive home. That's drinking and driving. But when they say to us, don't do it, we say,
but you do it, and they say, that's different.*
—Lucius, 15

*I'm glad you don't do drugs. I know I never will
after seeing what it did to my daddy. He's dead
from drugs. So, I hope you never do drugs.*
                              —Clarissa, 14

*My daddy does cocaine every single day. He sees
these commercials on TV about cocaine, but all
he says is it can't happen to me. Just the other
day he took all the money out of the bank, and
the water and the gas was turned off for a long
time. We had to boil water to keep warm and to
wash up in. Now we have no money and who
knows what he'll do next.*
                              —Janey, 11

*There was a family up the street from me whose
parents was on drugs and alcohol. It is so easy
to get drugs. They are all over the place.*
                              —Elena, 12

*I have a mother. She's okay, I guess, except she
smokes.*
                              —Kenley, 13

Here's the obligatory "Cosby Show" reference.

We did a show once where somebody put a joint between the pages in one of Theo's books. Remember? Of
course, Theo came home and his mother found the joint,
and she told Cliff, and the two of them sat Theo down for
a serious talk. They were upset, but they weren't exactly
mad, at least not yet; they were waiting to hear Theo's side
of the story before getting too emotional. He insisted the
joint wasn't his. (It wasn't.) He insisted he didn't know how
it got there. (He didn't.) His folks trusted him, but they
only half-believed him. They were willing to let it go, on
Theo's word, but Theo couldn't get rid of the feeling that

he'd let them down. He was determined to prove himself right, at all costs, and so he went back to school, and he found out who put the joint in his book, and then he dragged the kid back home to prove his point.

Now, I don't know about you, but that strikes me as a little unrealistic. What happened was that Theo confronted this guy and said, "Listen, you're going to come home with me and you're going to tell my parents what happened." The guy said, "No way," and he and Theo went back and forth about things for a while. You don't see them resolve the situation on the show, but you do see the guy go home with Theo, so figure it out. Theo kind of bullied him into it. I don't know any real-life situations where anything close to that would happen. Yeah, some guy's going to go over to your house and tell your mom and dad that the drugs they found in your book were his. Give me a break.

But the reason I mention that story is not to show how unrealistic it was, but to show you how our thinking has changed in the past decade or so, and to show you how the props of growing up have changed too. That episode was really only a carbon copy, with a twist, of a "Brady Bunch" episode from the early 1970s. In that one, the mother found a pack of cigarettes in her son's jacket. You remember that episode, the one where the pack slips out of Greg's pocket during an antismoking meeting his mother was hosting at the house. Greg's folks sat him down for a serious talk. He insisted the cigarettes weren't his. (They weren't.) He insisted he didn't know how they got there. (He didn't.) His parents trusted him the same way the Huxtables trusted Theo, but they also only half-believed he was telling the truth. They were also willing to let it go, on Greg's word, but Greg couldn't get rid of the feeling that he'd let them down.

Later on it turned out that Greg took home the wrong jacket from school (those varsity jackets all look the same!)

and that the pack of cigarettes belonged to a friend of his. He also took the friend home to explain the situation and to get him off the hook with his folks.

Okay, so we recycled an old idea. The message was the same, but we were reaching a whole different group of kids. What's interesting to me is the way the props were changed to reflect the times. It's as if we have to increase the artillery to get the same point across. A pack of cigarettes today doesn't mean the same thing it did ten years ago; for all I know a joint won't mean the same thing ten years from now that it does today. Maybe ten years from now we'll have gotten to the point where the same message could only be sent with a misplaced syringe and some rubber tubing.

That's sad.

I'm worried about a friend of mine who's into drugs and alcohol and even crack. She does them, a little, but I'm worried that her other friends are going to lead her into abusing them. Like this weekend, she's going out with some of her wild friends, and I'm scared for her.
—Cindy, 14

When I turned sixteen a new world was opened to me. I was bombarded with unsupervised parties and other situations where I was required to use my own judgment. I wanted to fit in so I started drinking some.
—Karen, 17

My friends made me try pot. We were driving and they locked the doors and blew the smoke in my face. It wasn't bad, like I thought it would be, but I'm mad that they decided everything for me.
—Scott, 15

★ 184 ★

I have a friend who has a drug problem. She says that smoking cigarettes and drinking alcohol are not examples of drug abuse but I told her to wake up and smell the coffee. I wonder what her problem is. Is she under peer pressure? I hope not.

—Roberto, 16

This notion of peer pressure as a kind of hypnotic state doesn't sit so well with me. I see it in a lot of letters, and I see it with a lot of kids I know, and I think I see it so much because of the pervasive media campaigns I talked about earlier. Again, this is what happens when a bust-out media-awareness campaign gets out of control. Madison Avenue has got us thinking that the only kids who drink or do drugs are those who fall under this spell cast by their drinking and drug-doing friends. They make it sound as if "peer pressure" is itself a drug, the one kids should most avoid taking.

Wrong. *Peer pressure* is an unfortunate term. For one thing, most times no "pressure," real or imagined, is ever directly applied; for another, any pressure that is indirectly applied is usually self-inflicted, but we tend to blame it on our peers. Peer pressure is the umbrella under which we do things we think we're supposed to be doing, or things other kids are doing, or things we'd like to be doing but don't feel strongly about unless everybody else is also doing them. It's a pressure we put on ourselves. We try to second-guess what's expected of us, and in our efforts to be liked and to fit in, we try anything.

Now, don't get me wrong. There are very real and very direct pressures facing almost every kid growing up today. There are also very real and very direct temptations out there for kids. I can certainly see the temptation to do things to show you belong, to show you're grown up. I can understand how a kid who's unsure of himself would want to experiment with drugs or alcohol, particularly if he

★ 185 ★

thought the experimenting would make him more popular. I can understand how a kid can seek to fit himself in by doing things he doesn't really believe in. We all put a lot of weight on appearances, but nobody sits us down and tells us what those appearances should be. And the kicker is, those attitudes about appearance change not only from one school to the next and from one group of kids to the next, but from one day to the next. What's in today is out tomorrow; what's cool tomorrow is lukewarm the day after next. This is what it's like for all of us, as far as drugs are concerned and as far as everything else is concerned.

For as far back as anyone can remember, the easiest, most surefire way to make friends and bolster your reputation has been to defy authority. For a kid who's looking to make a name for himself, there's nothing like doing what he's been specifically told not to do. And for a lot of kids, in a lot of schools, fitting in by defying your parents, your teachers, and other adults often starts with smoking cigarettes.

> *My friend Petra smokes cigarettes. She's only 15. In her sweaters she has holes that come from the cigarettes. The cigarettes make her breath smell and her body smell.*
> *—Tracy, 14*

> *I heard at school in my* Weekly Reader *that you are in a tape that tells you not to smoke. My dad used to smoke. But he stopped. I don't think I will ever smoke. I hope you don't.*
> *—Bruce, 8*

> *The first time me and my friend smoked we practiced by ourselves, because of the coughing, because we didn't want our friends to think we never smoked before. We did it in front of a*

*mirror at her parents' house. It took like three
or four times.*

—Harlene, 12

I'm not saying that smoking cigarettes leads to drug
and alcohol abuse. That's a line you hear all the time, but
I don't buy that. One doesn't necessarily lead to the other,
but they do tend to follow each other. What I mean is, the
kind of kid who teaches himself to pick up cigarettes as a
habit is the same kind of kid who starts drinking or smoking dope sooner than other kids. The same thinking that
gets him started smoking cigarettes also gets him going
in these other directions. It's not a cause-and-effect situation, not at all; it's just that the kids I know who drink
heavily, or who smoke dope, also tend to smoke cigarettes.
The two tend to go together. Think about the people you
know who drink or do drugs and see if you don't notice the
same thing.

It's amazing to me that, even with all the documented
evidence against it, kids still start smoking. It's not an
easy habit to pick up—you have to work at it—and yet kids
are still coughing their way through their first cigarettes
to look cool, or at least to work at looking cool. They're also
sucking back their first beers and wine coolers and whis-
key sours for the same reasons.

(I would be remiss if I did not remind you here that
cigarette smoke, alcohol, and drugs are hazardous to your
health. Forgive me if I sound like a broken record.)

*When school started in September I said to my-
self, "Well, I guess I'll go to all of my classes and
get straight As." But as it turned out I was on
the football team and we got drunk every day
and when grades came out I got straight Fs, or
just about.*

—Terry, 17

I would say that approximately eighty-five percent of the individuals I know have at least tried pot. As for drinking, everybody's doing it, from the cheerleaders to the rebels, to the straight-A students. Parents can't understand this.

—Joey, 16

I have a friend who's an alcoholic. He's my best friend's brother and I sort of think of him as a brother too. I'm really afraid for him because he's one that thinks he can drink and drive. Also, he's getting my best friend, his sister, to start drinking too. So now instead of one friend to worry about I have two.

—Alicia, 17

My brother is an alcoholic and sometimes he has hit me or my friends. Once, he came home drunk, and after fifteen minutes of trying to get him out of the car and into the house we hurried to brush his teeth and get him to bed before my parents came home.

—Patty, 15

My cousin lies to her mom and dad and tells them she's going to the movies with friends when really she goes to parties and gets so drunk that she can't find her way home and she'll have to spend the night. I miss those times when we would stay up talking for hours about family problems or problems at school or whatever, but that is all different now.

—Dilma, 14

Sometimes it seems there is not a single teenager left who does not drink. Well, it is not true.

I have survived the pressures of alcohol. Believe me, it is difficult at first, but it can be done. Before taking that first drink, stop and think about it. Ask yourself, is it really worth being a part of the group?

—Jack, 16

I don't smoke. I don't get drunk. I don't take drugs. Never have, never will. Mostly it's because I'm scared. I'm worried about the before-, during-, and aftereffects. I'm worried about what drugs would do to my chromosomes, and to my chromosomes' chromosomes. I'm worried about how I'd handle it all. I guess those scare-tactic awareness campaigns have done a number on me, because I avoid the stuff like the plague. Besides, I could never understand the fun or the joy in doing drugs or getting drunk. They don't offer me anything I'm not able to get in some other way. I'm able to go and hang out with my friends and just be real wild without getting drunk or stoned. I'm sure people have seen me and my friends out in public and thought we were on something, because we can get pretty crazy sometimes.

Since I've been doing "Cosby," it's been much easier for me to stand up for what I believe is right, and to speak out against what I believe is wrong. Drugs are wrong. Just saying no, for me, is a lot easier than it is for most kids, because I already have an image and a reputation to fall back on. As I mentioned elsewhere in this book, I'm a lot more self-confident than I've ever been before. Now, when I walk down the street and someone comes up to me and says, "Yo, man, try these, try these," I can say, "Step off! I'm not with that!" Today something like that would be water off my back, but a few years ago I could see that I might have had some trouble with it.

I know some people who smoke dope, some even who do crack or coke—I think every kid does—but if they want to mess up their lives like that there's nothing I can do about it. I'm not into preaching to my friends. That's one quick way to lose your friends. All of my good friends, though, feel the same way I do, and so there's no need to preach.

Sometimes I wonder how I'd handle the temptations to do drugs if I were in a regular school, if I were the kind of "regular people" Theo talks about on the show. I think I'd still be all right, as far as this goes, but I can't be sure. Things would be tougher for me; I know that. I know they must be tough for you. It's hard, I know, to do what you think is right when all around you everyone is coaching you to do something you think is wrong. There are no easy ways around that.

I hear from a lot of kids with a lot to say about a lot of this. Listen up and I'll shut up, at least for the next few pages:

> *I'm in a Just Say No club. I write plays and then I get kids to help me do them. I just wrote one about a boy that gets offered drugs. I hope when I present it the kids will enjoy it but also learn something. Well, I guess that's all.*
> *—Tasha, 14*

> *I try to help kids out with this drug kick. I know I'm not a person to try to set examples, but I hate to see kids messing their lives up with drugs.*
> *—Darla, 15*

> *Make sure you get a good education and stay drug-free because WE ARE THE FUTURE.*
> *—Derrick, 12*

> *I'm glad you don't do drugs. That's so dumb it makes me sick when I hear about crack, cocaine, etc., on TV. I say to myself, those people*

just don't know what they're doing, not only are they killing themselves but also the people that love them. Malcolm, I just don't understand it. It's really pathetic.

—Kristy, 17

Last year a girl at my school was killed by a drunk driver. For all I know, I could be next.

—Alba, 14

I don't do well. I've been held back once, almost twice but teachers didn't like me so much they passed me even though I made straight Fs. They didn't want me in their class anymore. I've been to a juvenile detention hall once and no one knows about it. When I was 10 I was living the life of a 14-year-old, and now I'm 14 and I'm living the life of a 16-year-old. Now my life is good and I'm off drugs and I just quit smoking about six months ago.

—Bradley, 14

If I am friends with someone and I find out they do drugs, I ignore them, but my preacher told me to stay friends with them because they might need me and they might need my friends too.

—Caroline

My brother was doing drugs and he told me if I told my parents he would do something drastic if I told. But then I told anyway and my brother got real mad at me then. I was talking to him one night and I was crying real bad and I told him I didn't want to be like him and waste my life. He said he wasn't wasting his. But you

know and I know that anyone on drugs is wasting their life.
                                    —*Teresa, 13*

Let me just slip in a word about drugs and teen violence, because the two tend to go hand in hand. A good percentage of conflicts among kids has to do with drugs or alcohol, or at least they occur under the influence of drugs or alcohol. The stuff just clouds your mind so that you start doing things you wouldn't otherwise start doing. Think about it: does it make any kind of sense to bash in a car window, to spray paint your name on a building, or to tear down a street sign? No, it doesn't, but when you're not thinking straight, things start to look a little different.

I have a bad habit. I have trouble keeping out of trouble. I am always getting into things with my friends, drugs and other things. They talk me into the most treacherous things.
                                    —*Peter, 15*

I will not drink until I'm older, and I'm not going to take drugs if at all until I'm older because I know how they screw up your body.
                                    —*Alexander, 13*

Saying no to drugs will always be hard because kids want to try different things. But it gets easier every day.
                                    —*Brandon, 16*

Ads say, "Friends don't let friends drive drunk," but when a friend won't give you the keys and really gets mad when you ask for them, what do you do?
                                    —*Arianne, 16*

When I was a sophomore the drug dealers were known by their Gucci sweatshirts. I myself have been confronted three times to use drugs. The reason that number is so low is because I am a double varsity letterman and am fairly popular. People know how I feel.

—Claudell, 17

I know you're really against drugs, and I just want to say I've never tried them, and never will. I've been offered them at parties and at school, but I just said no.

—Nadine, 15

When I was in junior high, a girl who had been my baby-sitter was hit by a drunk driver and died immediately. My mother also was in a drinking-related accident. It gets me so mad. Here we are, 16 and 17 years old, and we're drinking and driving all over the place. I don't know what to do about it.

—Kanda, 16

In my school you sometimes see needles in the bathrooms. Not all the time, though. Most of the time you just see beer cans and cigarette butts and roaches. It's amazing what goes on in there. They say the boys' bathroom is even worse.

—Marcella, 15

I am one of three girls in a committee against drugs for our school paper. We are writing about why you shouldn't deal with drugs or with people who deal with drugs. We are trying to really get to the students. Will you tell your opinion on that?

—Elise, 11

★ 193 ★

Everyone at school knows which people use drugs. The administration knows drugs are being used in the parking lot during school, but they just turn away and ignore it. I think the problem begins with younger kids. My brother is in eighth grade, but has been exposed to drugs at his school since sixth grade. At that age and maturity level it is cool to use drugs. Can you believe it?
                                              —Timothy, 16

This guy Timothy has hit on something here and it scares me to think about it. Kids are confronting the complicated issues surrounding drugs and alcohol at an earlier and earlier age than ever before. I don't know why that's the case, but it is. It used to be that the subject came up only in high school, and then it started turning up in junior high school, and now it's right smack in the middle of the fifth and sixth grades. It's creeping back and back, and at this rate eventually kids will be exposed to the stuff before they're even born. (Actually, they are; more and more babies are born addicted to the stuff because their moms are addicted to the stuff.)

It disturbs me when I get letters from kids who should have other things on their minds.

Why do drugs cost so much? I mean you could go to a drugstore and buy medicine.
                                              —Christina, 7

My father keeps his joints in a cigarette box in one of his jacket pockets. He thinks we don't know about them, but we know about them.
                                              —Jennifer, 7

Do you think we should take drugs? Me and you shouldn't take drugs.

—Jason, 6

Six years old! Can you believe that?

Mostly, though, the letters I get on this subject are from older kids. Occasionally, I'll hear from one who's really given this problem some thought.

Why don't they just take all the drugs away to a place and burn them and put all the people who try to sell them into jail someplace? It's not our fault that we do them if they're so easy to get.

—Carlos

I say no when people ask me to get high with them, except the reason I give is that I'm allergic to smoke. That's not really the reason.

—Ricanne, 16

A way to stop people from bringing drugs into schools is to hire guards and put them in front of the school. They could also stop people from doing drugs.

—Jeffrey, 15

What do they expect? We're just kids.

—Holly, 15

As I said earlier, I do get involved in the "Just Say No!" programs around the country. I want to help; it's just that I don't always know how helpful I can be, or how helpful I'm allowed to be. I appeared at one of their press conferences once, in Washington, D.C., and a kid from one of the local high schools brought up a good point. He

★ 195 ★

echoed one of the earlier letters and said, "Why are you putting the pressure on us kids to just say no? Why don't you crack down on the people who are bringing the drugs into this country?"

I never thought about things in just that way before, but it makes sense to me. Here we are spending all this money and energy on a "Just Say No!" campaign that can only be so successful. I'm not saying we should cut back on our effort there, no way, but if we really want to get at the problem of substance abuse among our young people we should be equally committed to coming at it from other directions.

I'm open for suggestions.

15

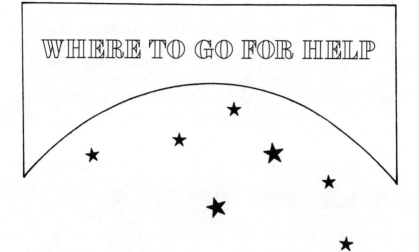

WHERE TO GO FOR HELP

NOTES ON RESOURCES

*I need to know a place where kids can go to talk
about their problems.*

—Ellis, 14

There are a lot of people and agencies better qualified than
I to help you, or your child, over a few rough spots. There
are other books, too, which go into much deeper and richer
detail on some of the subjects touched on here.

*Remember, this book is intended only to reflect
what kids are going through today.* As I said at the beginning, I'm not in any position to do much more than relate
what it is I'm going through, or what my friends are going
through, or what the kids who write to me are going

through. I can't do much more than that, or at least I shouldn't.

But much more is needed, and so here are some good places to start:

First of all, pick up any book by Judy Blume (*Are You There God? It's Me, Margaret; Tiger Eyes; Blubber;* and others). Then read it. No other author writes about kids, for kids, with as much wit, intelligence, and feeling. She writes about love and friendship and school and family; her stories, all of them, can make you feel better about yourself, and they can teach you things about yourself and about the world you live in. Also, they almost always seem to be about you, or at least they almost always seem to be about me.

If you're a little bit older, you might try something by S. E. Hinton. Her books (*The Outsiders; That Was Then, This Is Now;* and others) have also been around for a generation now, and she also writes about the pain of growing up and the struggle to fit in. Check her out.

Parents, get your hands on almost anything by Earl A. Grollman. He's written some wonderful books (on suicide, death, and divorce, among other topics), published by Beacon Press, to help you and your kids get past some trouble spots. They may be hard to find, but they're worth seeking out.

For kids, and parents, interested in reading more about suicide and depression, I'd recommend *Vivienne: The Life and Suicide of an Adolescent Girl,* by John Mack and Holly Hickler (New American Library), and *Too Young to Die,* by Francine Klagsbrun (Pocket Books). Both will set you straight on a few things, and help you to feel the despair of adolescent depression in a new way. Another wonderful book is *A Cry for Help,* by Mary Giffin and Carol Felsenthal (Doubleday).

If you're feeling depressed or suicidal, or, parents, if you're worried about your child, you can contact the American Association of Suicidology (2459 S. Ash Street,

Denver, CO 80222; 303-692-0985). They're a nonprofit group whose goal is to understand and prevent suicide. They also serve as a national clearinghouse for information and resources on suicide and depression, so they can refer you to a hotline or suicide-prevention program in your area. Call them. They're there to help. Or, call directory assistance for the number of a hotline/helpline in your area; it should be listed under "Suicide."

Kids in trouble, and parents with troubled kids, can also contact The National Network of Runaway and Youth Services, Inc. (905 6th Street, SW, Suite 411, Washington, DC 20024; 202-488-0739). They're supported by the National Fund for Runaway Children (if you'd like to contribute, write to P.O. Box 70250, Washington, DC 20024), and it's their job to promote awareness of runaway services, and to steer runaway kids in the right direction.

There are several national toll-free numbers you can call:

—The Runaway Switchboard (1-800-621-4000)

—The National Runaway Hotline (1-800-231-6946)

—Home Run (1-800-448-4663)

—The Covenant House Nine Line (1-800-999-9999)

If you need someone to talk to, about anything, you'll find someone at those numbers twenty-four hours a day, seven days a week. Each of the numbers is set up to help runaway kids. That's their focus, but they'll field calls about almost any problem. They can answer questions, or just listen. Make use of them. For any reason. Parents, the hotlines also serve as bulletin boards; that means you can sometimes get a message to your kid through their switchboard. Call them if you think your child is in any kind of trouble.

We talked earlier about how most kids who leave home are running away from serious family problems. Well, the Childhelp National Child Abuse Hotline (1-800-422-4453) can help talk you through an abusive situation at home and they can recommend local agencies who can offer additional help. Call them if there's even a hint of trouble; they're also there around the clock.

Parents in trouble can find help at Parents Anonymous (6733 S. Sepulveda Boulevard, Suite 270, Los Angeles, CA 90045; 213-410-9732). They're a national help network for abusive or potentially abusive parents, with regional offices and support groups all across the country. Some local chapters also offer programs and support groups for teenagers and younger children. They do nice work.

For trouble in "blended" families, you might contact The Step-Family Association of America (602 E. Joppa Road, Baltimore, MD 21204; 301-823-7570), a national support group for stepfamilies or soon-to-be stepfamilies. They have about sixty chapters around the country, and they publish a helpful newsletter for members. They also provide a book club service to members, through which they make available such wonderful books as *Stepdog,* by Marlene Fanta Shyer, a book for kids looking at stepfamilies from a pet's perspective, and *Remarriage: A Family Affair,* by Lillian Messenger, an adult look at overcoming the conflicts and headaches of stepfamilies.

If moving to a new school or town has got you down and out, turn to *The Teenager's Survival Guide to Moving,* by W. M. Heller and P. C. Nida. It's one of the few books I could find on the subject, but even in a more crowded field it would still be one of the best. Also, a guidance counselor at your new school should be able to refer you to local programs and activities to help you get acquainted with your new community. Ask; that's what they're there for.

If you'd like to get involved in issues of race and race relations in your community, or if you have some questions that need answering, get in touch with the NAACP's national office (4805 Mount Hope Drive, Baltimore, MD 21215; 301-358-8900). They have a lot of good programs for kids and they can steer you to a lot of useful resources. Direct your questions to the Youth and College Division. The National Association for the Advancement of Colored People has regional offices in New York, Atlanta, San Francisco, Detroit, Dallas, and St. Louis, and local chapters throughout the country. Or, call the Urban League in your area; they're listed. Also, read *The Nature of Prejudice*, by Gordon Allport (Addison-Wesley); it tells you what you need to know.

Planned Parenthood (810 Seventh Avenue, New York, NY 10019; 212-541-7800) is still the single best place to turn for questions about sex and sexuality. Write to the director of education for further information. Planned Parenthood has a terrific Adolescent Pregnancy Prevention Campaign, which can get you all the facts and shatter all the myths about birth control. They're really making a push in this area. If you're pregnant, or if you think you might be pregnant, or if you're not sure about the birth control method you're using, give a call. Check the phone book for the local chapter nearest you or call the national office. Many local chapters offer birth control and sex education classes in addition to one-on-one counseling.

Parents, a copy of a book called *Raising Your Child Conservatively in a Sexually Permissive World*, by Sol Gordon and Judith Gordon (Simon & Schuster), will help you send the right signals to your kids about sex.

If you've got a drinking problem, local chapters of Alcoholics Anonymous (P.O. Box 459, Grand Central Station, New York, NY 10163) can be found in almost every town. They're listed, and they're there to help you get your head on straight when you've admitted to yourself you're an alcoholic. Or, if there's a drinking problem in your family, you can get help for your family member, or for yourself, by contacting Al-Anon (World Service Headquarters, 1372 Broadway, New York, NY 10018; 1-800-356-9996, or 212-302-7240). They also reach into hundreds of communities around the country, and many local chapters offer specific programs, such as Alateen, for the children and siblings of alcoholics.

Similarly, Narcotics Anonymous chapters turn up in most of our big cities. They'll help you kick the drug habit, whatever the drug and whatever the habit. Check your local phone books. Also, Nar-Anon (P.O. Box 2562, Palos Verdes Peninsula, CA 90274; 213-547-5800) is there to help the families of drug users. They're set up in pretty much the same way as Al-Anon, although they're not affiliated in any way. Parents, you can find Nar-Anon chapters in most metropolitan areas, and they'll help you to help your kids. In some cities, Nar-Anon also has programs for siblings and children of drug users: Narateen (for kids ages eleven to seventeen) and Preteen (for kids five to eleven). Call the chapters in your area to see what programs are available.

The best resource I could find to help you through the loss of a friend or a loved one is The Good Grief Program (295 Longwood Avenue, Boston, MA 02115; 617-232-8390). It's part of the Judge Baker Children's Center, a local children's mental-health agency which is the home base of my friend Dr. Alvin Poussaint; they also offer reach-out and referral services nationally. Let them help you.

A final note: The Children's Defense Fund (122 C Street, NW, Washington, DC 20001; 202-628-8787) is a nonprofit children's advocacy group based in our nation's capital. They monitor congressional activities as they relate to children, and they lobby Congress on such issues as child welfare and adolescent pregnancy prevention. All social programs and policies relating to children are monitored through their offices. Don't call them for hotline or helpline advice, but do call them for a national voice (and a national ear). They do some wonderful work; if you'd like to make a donation, you can write to the address given.

JUST ONE MORE THING

You know, I've just read through this entire book, as I hope you have at this point, and it leaves me feeling as if I've just stayed up all night talking about anything and everything with a really good friend. I suppose, for me, that really good friend is you. I hope, for you, that I've been able to be the same good friend to you. I also hope you continue to find a friend in Theo Huxtable. It's funny, but Theo's a good friend of mine too. People don't usually think of an actor befriending the character he plays, but that's the way I feel sometimes. I'm drawn to the same qualities of his that you are. I'll miss him when he disappears from my life, just as I'll miss all of you (and your letters) when you disappear along with him.

For now, though, I'm glad we had this chance to get together and go over this stuff. We've covered some things that are hard to talk about and some things that are easy to talk about. Some of it was funny, some of it was sad, but all of it was important. All of it fits somehow into the growing up we do every day.

We'll have to do it again sometime.

AFTERWORD

Malcolm, a teenager himself, has taken on the difficult challenge of responding to the hopes, interests, and conflicts of his fellow adolescents. In so doing, he proves to be sensitive, thoughtful, insightful, and a very good listener. From a professional point of view, I find the words of encouragement and advice that he offers to young people to be surprisingly sound. Malcolm has become a first-rate "peer counselor" in a role that has been thrust upon him.

I recommend this volume as a helpful handbook for teenagers and their parents. I think that teenagers particularly will find it useful because it is written in language they understand; the voices that emerge from the letters are those of people very much like themselves, dealing with problems many of them can identify with. Malcolm, as one of them, draws on many of his own growing-up experiences to reach out to his fellow teens, and to establish trust with them. He, therefore, has a great advantage over the so-called experts on adolescent behavior.

But what is most impressive about his approach is that, most of the time, Malcolm takes definitive stands on controversial issues. He obviously lives by a clear and positive value system, and he is not embarrassed to assert it. For the most part, his values are those that psychiatrists, psychologists, and educators would confirm as being appropriate for the healthy and safe development for most teenagers in today's world.

What is a teenager, anyway? And why all the fuss and worry about this passing stage of the life cycle? Some reasons are obvious. This is the period of life in which physical and psychological growth occur most rapidly. It is a time of awakening sexuality and the appearance of secondary sex characteristics, resulting from the body's production of certain hormones. Their developing interest in the opposite sex and acceleration of physical growth can be staggering enough for many young people to deal with. But added to that are concerns about the self, and the need for the approval of friends, that increase in intensity as teenagers try to understand who and what they are. At this stage, most young people begin to think independently and abstractly. They want things to make sense to them in their own terms, and some of them are more concerned with social and moral issues than many adults. Their minds, thankfully, are often both fresh and refreshing.

Teenagers present a real challenge, because they tend to resist parental and adult advice and turn to their friends for counsel and direction. Adolescents have a strong need to belong and to be accepted by those they identify as their peer group. They require this group support in order to experiment with life and new ideas, and they need the understanding of people like themselves as they make the voyage toward the greater psychological independence that we call adulthood.

It is essential to keep in mind the great degree of variability that marks the rate of passage through the teen years. For instance, many girls begin to menstruate at the age of ten or eleven, others at fourteen or fifteen. Some young people, owing to their particular environment, are given a great deal of responsibility in their early years; others may not have to assume adult duties until they are well into their twenties. For many, the teen years are marred by the harsh realities of poverty, poor schools,